D0332461

PHOTOGRAPHERS' BRITAIN

THE HIGHLANDS

For Tom and Margaret

PHOTOGRAPHERS' BRITAIN

THE HIGHLANDS

DAVID PATERSON

ALAN SUTTON

First published in the United Kingdom in 1993
Alan Sutton Publishing Ltd · Phoenix Mill · Far Thrupp · Stroud · Gloucestershire

First published in the United States of America in 1993
Alan Sutton Publishing Inc. · 83 Washington Street · Dover NH 03820

British Library Cataloguing in Publication Data applied for

Paterson, David
Photographers' Britain: The Highlands
I. Title

ISBN 0-7509 0159-4

Library of Congress Cataloging in Publication Data applied for

Cover photograph: Buachaille Etive Mor, Glencoe
Title page photograph: Cow and calf at Dounreay, Caithness

Typeset in 10/14 Sabon.
Typesetting and origination by
Alan Sutton Publishing Limited.
Printed in Great Britain by
The Bath Press, Avon.

INTRODUCTION

My connections with the Highlands are long and deep, though I have spent most of my life, and all my adult years, living outside them. My father's career in teaching took us, in 1951 when I was six, to Golspie on the east coast of Sutherland. For the first year we lived in the schoolhouse in the hamlet of Loth, some 20 km up the coast, and while my father commuted each day to and from Golspie, I went to the tiny village school next door, where a dozen or so children of all ages shared one classroom and one teacher. My memories of that childhood year in Loth are extremely warm, and the experience of village life and the freedom we children had to explore and enjoy our environment lie behind my great love of nature and the Highlands. For the rest of my school years we lived in Golspie (my parents are still there) and, though the community was bigger, our surroundings were no less beautiful; my holidays were spent in the hills and woods around the village, or on the miles of unspoilt beach which began just a hundred metres from our house. Teenage years, however, were spent doing things other than enjoying nature, and for a time the landscape held no interest for me, until after leaving university I discovered photography. Simultaneously, I renewed my acquaintance with the Highlands and began a life-long love affair with them. For the next eighteen years I lived mainly in Edinburgh, and spent most spare time in the hills, walking, skiing, climbing and photographing; since moving to London in 1983 my trips north have been only a little less frequent. We have a house at Morar in west Inverness-shire, and I spend a good deal of time there, mostly in the winter months, getting to know another part of the Highlands better. Back in London, hardly a day passes when I am not planning journeys, climbs and photographic trips, and most of the schemes involve the north of Scotland, somehow.

The Highlands constitute a land mass whose area is greater than that of Wales, with a western coastline more complex and riven with fjords than any other country except Norway. Highland Region contains some four hundred mountains which rise to 914 m

SRON NA CREISE, GLENCOE, IN WINTER

(3000 ft) or more, many hundreds of lesser hills, countless rivers, streams and lochs, and six large and numerous small islands; but hardly any people. The regional centre and largest town, Inverness, has less than forty thousand inhabitants, and the next four largest – Fort William, Wick, Thurso and Dingwall – together have less than thirty-five thousand. Most villages have under a thousand people, and where the land will not support agriculture, vast swathes of territory are completely empty. Northern Scotland is by far the most sparsely populated part of the British Isles, and this is one of its most obvious and abiding characteristics as you travel around the region.

The Highlands are unique in their blend of mountain, river, loch, sea and sky, and, though frequently uncertain, the weather plays a large part in enhancing the beauty of the landscapes. The Atlantic airstream brings constant change to the skies over northern Scotland, and a seemingly unending blanket of cloud can give way in moments to blue skies, and sunshine which sparkles from rock and stream. The shifting skies themselves are often of great beauty and, combined with a panorama of moorland and mountain, can create powerful images. Though the terrain throughout the region shares certain basic components, the scenery is extremely diverse, and there is little similarity between say, the massive rolling tops of the Cairngorms and the shattered, jagged ridges of the Cuillin of Skye. The coastline is equally varied, with massive cliffs, long and inhospitable rocky stretches, and startling white beaches of coral- or shell-sand. Add to these the sweeps of open moorland, the myriad lochs and rivers and the woods and forests alive with animal life and bird-song, and you have a landscape you will never tire of; certainly, I shall not.

I have photographed the Highlands since my earliest days with a camera, and a handful of the photographs in this collection date back to the early 1970s, though most are of recent origin. It was only when beginning to assemble existing material for this book that I realized how predominantly I had used colour to photograph the Scottish hills. Putting this balance right by taking many new pictures in black-and-white has been a great joy for me, and in some ways has helped me to rediscover black-and-white photography. I hope there will be some discoveries in these pages for you, too.

DAVID PATERSON
Tougal, Morar 1992

LOCH TULLA AND THE BLACKMOUNT

Only three roads penetrate Highland Region from the south, and the most spectacular of these winds its way up Loch Lomond side, through Glen Falloch and dramatic Strath Fillan to Loch Tulla, Rannoch Moor and finally Glencoe on the southern fringes of the Region.

On a crisp winter's day of deep blue skies and white peaks etched against the blue, when not a sound breaks the stillness, there is something quite magical about Loch Tulla and its hills. There are no houses to be seen, the main road is far enough away that the sound of traffic does not intrude, and there is a sublime combination of pine woods, water, mountain and sky. All this has a timeless quality which can make you feel that you have somehow stumbled on a landscape from deep in the past, or that what lies beyond the snow-covered hills is a thousand kilometres of trackless arctic tundra. In a sense both feelings have some accuracy, since with no visual reminders of the twentieth century, this looks very much as the Highlands did some centuries ago, before most of the deforestation occurred. Now, surviving pockets of these old woodlands always convey a sense of the past. Beyond the hills lies not Arctic tundra, but further range upon range of hills. The Scottish mountains have all been cut from an ancient tableland by the erosion of ice and water, and their summits, rising and falling like the wave crests of an ocean, are the surviving fragments of the surface of that high plateau. In today's climate these summits lie on the fringe of arctic conditions and are an echo of the distant past when all of this was deep-frozen tundra.

Loch Tulla lies just a kilometre or two south-west of the edge of Rannoch Moor, and shares the hills of the Blackmount as a backdrop. The old Glencoe road, avoiding the difficulties of the moor, ran around the western end of the loch from the old coaching inn at nearby Inveroran and under the rim of hills to the next stage at Kingshouse. Now it is a favourite footpath, as thousands of walkers annually tread the West Highland Way.

LOCHAN NA H'ACHLAISE AND RANNOCH MOOR

Beyond the miniature summits of Meall Mor and Meall Beag, the hills rising from the western edge of Rannoch Moor are hidden in the low clouds of a summer weather front. One of the great playgrounds of the Scottish mountains, known collectively as The Blackmount, these hills form one of the finest ranges in the west Highlands. With half a dozen summits of around 1070 m (3510 ft), the hills are high enough to attract and keep a large amount of snow throughout most winters and, though not known for extremely difficult routes, the range is very popular with walkers and climbers. On the eastern-most slopes of the group, on Meall a Bhuiridh, there is fine skiing at one of Scotland's longest-established pistes.

Rannoch Moor itself lies at around 300 m (980 ft) and is frequently snow-covered for long spells. Exposed to winds from any direction, the main road, beside which this photograph was taken, crosses the centre of the moor and is often closed by drifting snow, or passable only by convoys of vehicles headed by snow-ploughs.

Half a mile beyond the hills in the photograph, the West Highland Way follows the old Glencoe road across the western fringes of the moor. The track rises to a maximum height of around 460 m (1510 ft), and, on a winter's day with a wind blowing, it is a cold, remote stretch to have to cross. At other seasons, many walkers divert from the route to climb one of several peaks which are easily accessible from the trail. All of the summits of the Blackmount give fine views southwards across the moor, which on a summer's day sparkles everywhere with streams and lochans.

ROCK FORMATIONS, GLEN ETIVE

At the south-eastern end of Glencoe, a narrow road heads down into a deep valley between Buachaille Etive Mor, the most easterly of the Glencoe peaks, and Sron na Creise, the first of the Blackmount hills. This is Glen Etive, one of the finest of all the west Highland glens, and certainly one of the longest. The road snakes down the bottom of the valley for some 20 km, flanked on both sides by steep-sided mountains and in the lower end of the glen by forestry, until it reaches the head of Loch Etive. This is a sea loch, and again one of the longest and narrowest, twisting through the hills for another 30 km before reaching the sea to the north of Oban. Glen Etive has many attractions, not least its remoteness and wild scenery. There is also much wildlife, and large herds of red deer can be seen at various times of year but especially in winter when they come lower down to feed. Golden eagles inhabit the glen, and sea eagles, released into the wild as part of the reintroduction scheme centred on Rum, have been seen at the seaward end. The surrounding hills are all of great interest to hill-walkers, and rock-climbers come to Glen Etive for the massive sweep of granite slabs on the lower slopes of Ben Trilleachan, where much fine, delicate climbing is to be had on the smooth, almost holdless, rock. In the upper reaches of the glen, the River Etive runs for several kilometres through a rocky gorge, which, though not particularly deep, forces the river through a long succession of falls, rapids and narrows. The fast-flowing water has, over the ages, cut and smoothed the bedrock of beautiful pink granite into a great variety of fantastic shapes. The photograph was taken in winter; frost had glazed the rocks and a thin skin of ice covered the pools.

Sron na Creise and Buachaille Etive Mor

If you approach Glencoe from the south up the main A82 road, or on foot up the old military road, eventually you climb away from Rannoch Moor, and leave behind the infinite soft gradations of mountains and sky reflected in the moor's many lochans and watercourses. For a short time the view ahead is limited by rising ground, but as you come over a crest the Glencoe hills are suddenly spread before you in all their splendour, five or so kilometres away across open ground. It is an impressive introduction and, as you progress north-west into the Pass of Glencoe, though the scenery becomes ever wilder and steep-sided hills bristling with cliffs rise from both sides of the road, nothing else quite surpasses this first panorama. With their genius for giving the landscape the most poetic of names, the people of Glencoe called the finest of their mountains Buachaille Etive Mor – the Great Shepherd of Etive.

Glencoe is most famous, or infamous, for the massacre, the story of which barely needs to be retold. Conceived as an example to any other Highland clan that might be tempted to show less than total respect for the government in Edinburgh and London, the Macdonalds of Glencoe were to be slaughtered in a vile act of treachery. The deed was carried out by the Government's proxies in the Highlands, the Campbells, this time led by Campbell of Glenlyon. The order, issued by the Under Secretary of State, Sir William Dalrymple, instructed them that 'the manner of execution must be sure, secret and effectual' and that all under the age of seventy were to be put to the sword. In the event, some of the Campbell soldiers may not have had the stomach for the deed; warning hints were dropped and, of the two hundred or so Macdonalds living in the Glen forty were murdered, most of these being the elderly, the infirm and children. Perhaps as many more died of exposure in the snows of the surrounding hills and mountains. It was 12 February 1692, a date that will be remembered as long as Scotland survives.

In the aftermath the scandal was concealed. The King, who had signed the papers, escaped all censure, as did Campbell of Glenlyon and his troops. Sir William Dalrymple was dismissed from his post. But for the Macdonalds it was the end. Scattered throughout the region, with homes and byres destroyed and burned, cattle driven off or killed, and nearly half the clan dead, they never reclaimed their old lands in Glencoe.

GLENCOE VILLAGE

At the lower end of Glencoe, where the valley turns a corner and narrows, the River Coe runs for 3 km through a very pleasant wooded stretch with a minor road along its banks. Quite suddenly the road takes you over a little bridge and you find yourself in Glencoe village. Although it was in this very part of the Glen and in the village itself where the worst of the massacre occurred, time has healed at least the physical scars and there is little in the way of ruins or any other direct evidence left. What there is, the Glencoe Folk Museum in nearby Ballachulish, which shows scenes of restored crofts and items from former agricultural and slate industries, has in its collection of Macdonald and Jacobite relics. The village itself is a thriving centre now, busy through the summer months with the tourist trade, and all year round with walkers and climbers who congregate in ever greater numbers. The wild Glencoe hills are what draws them and, though the village and its hinterland are well supplied with b&bs, bunkhouses and so on, at any season there will be a rash of tents pitched up and down the Glen, but especially around the Clachaig Inn, whose public bar is the traditional haunt of the Glencoe climber.

Glencoe village has a superb setting, hemmed in by the peaks at the western mouth of the valley, with the river running deep and slow at the end of the main street, and woods and forest climbing the lower slopes of the hills. In the photograph, looking east, Sgurr nam Fiannadh gleams with a covering of fresh snow. This mountain, together with the rest of the superb Glencoe range, has been preserved for public use by the National Trust, which owns almost 6000 hectares including all the highest peaks and the magnificent Aonach Eagach ridge, which terminates above the village at Sgurr nam Fiannadh.

CASTLE STALKER, PORTNACROISH

West of Glencoe, the coast road from Oban to Fort William runs up the shores of Loch Linnhe, and just to the north of the long and beautiful island of Lismore, one of Scotland's most atmospheric castles sits on a tiny island a couple of hundred metres from the stony beach. Formerly a ruin but now restored, Castle Stalker (Falconer's Castle) was built in the sixteenth century by the Stewarts of Appin and is a typical fortified tower house of that period (other similar ones are Kisimul Castle, on the island of Barra, and Castle Tioram, further north near Kinlochmoidart). The Stewart name is that of the former Kings of Scotland, and this branch of the family suffered greatly in the aftermath of the terrible defeat at the battle of Culloden during the 1745 rebellion. Stewart of Ardsheal was forced into exile for his part in the uprising and for his role at Culloden itself where he led the clan into battle. Cumberland's army, in its later depredations, drove Stewart's wife and children from their home, and the whole of Appin received cruel treatment at the hands of the Government and their agents, clan Campbell, for their loyalty to the House of Stewart.

In 1751 a notorious incident occurred which was later used by R.L. Stevenson in his novel *Kidnapped*. This was the 'Appin Murder'. A local man, James Stewart, known as James of the Glens, was evicted from his land by the estate factor, Colin Campbell of Glenure, because of his Jacobite sympathies. Later, Campbell of Glenure was fatally shot not far away. Though the known culprit had escaped, James of the Glens was arrested, charged with the murder and tried before a Campbell judge and jury. He was found guilty, executed at Ballachulish and his corpse left to hang in chains for many years as a grisly reminder to all Stewarts.

LOCH LINNHE AT AUCHINTORE

On a fine evening in early summer, twilight glimmered across the placid waters of Loch Linnhe on the outskirts of Fort William. This lovely sea loch stretches nearly 60 km from Fort William to where its waters mingle with those of the Firth of Lorne, beyond Lismore Island. It is one of the longest sea lochs in Scotland, and if the Firth of Lorne – a narrow channel between the Isle of Mull and the mainland – is included, it is more than 70 km before the open sea is reached, somewhere south of Mull. Inland from Fort William, Loch Linnhe turns abruptly westwards, changes its name to Loch Eil and forges another 15 km into the hills. Its importance as a waterway reaching so far inland was recognized early and was no doubt a deciding factor in positioning the original fort here. For the same reason the Caledonian Canal was conceived and built, to take advantage of this natural passage to shipping which penetrates to the half-way point between open water on the east and west coasts. The canal's western terminus is on the shores of Loch Linnhe opposite Fort William, at Corpach, and the most impressive feature of the entire canal – a series of locks known as Neptune's Staircase – climbs immediately away from the terminus. Built by Thomas Telford, the canal was started in 1803 and took forty-four years to complete, having a total of twenty-nine locks and 35 km of actual canal linking the lochs of the Great Glen. Telford was also responsible for building, in the first years of the nineteenth century, the romantic 'Road to the Isles' which runs along the shores of Loch Linnhe's western branch, Loch Eil. Fort William's main road communications towards Glasgow, Stirling and Edinburgh run down the east side of Loch Linnhe, and 15 km from the town the loch is crossed by a small car ferry, at Corran.

Corran Ferry is the last of several that used to cross the mouths of some of Scotland's west-coast fjords. At nearby Ballachulish, Connell in Argyl, Kylestrome in Wester Ross and Kylescue in Sutherland car ferries used to add great charm, though sometimes long delays, to journeys up and down the coast. Today, all the others have been bridged or bypassed, and only Corran survives as a reminder of the days of more leisurely motoring, when getting out of the car to stretch your legs as you waited 20 minutes or so for the ferry was all part of the pleasure of travelling.

BEN NEVIS FROM THE CORPACH BASIN

The Caledonian Canal reaches its western terminus at Corpach, opposite Fort William on the shores of Loch Linnhe. Of all the views of Ben Nevis, the traditional view from Corpach must be one of the finest, though nothing of the great north face can be seen. Instead, the massive bulk of the mountain clearly shows, dwarfing the tiny houses of Fort William at the right-hand edge of the photograph. Even on a fine winter's day, Ben Nevis is rarely free from cloud, and during the twenty-one years when a weather observatory operated on the summit it was found that the mountain only received one-sixth of the possible hours of sunshine.

The village of Corpach grew rapidly after the establishment of a wood-pulp and paper-making mill there during the early 1970s. The pulp mill is still there, but paper-making ceased some years ago. The extra costs involved in operating so far from suppliers and markets has made it difficult to run major manufacturing industries successfully in the Highlands, and the Corpach paper mill is only one of the casualties of recent years, when a harder eye was cast on subsidies and support for regional industry.

The fishing boat lying in the Corpach basin has come through the Caledonian Canal from Inverness, 100 km away. A steady trickle of boats like this still use the canal to get to and from their home ports along the Moray Firth, when they want to fish in west-coast waters, but the major users of the canal are yacht and pleasure-boat owners who cruise the lochs of the Great Glen. Linked by the canal, the lochs provide a huge area of safe water to cruise and explore, and boat charter is a significant local industry.

GLENLOCHY DISTILLERY, FORT WILLIAM

There is a history of whisky-making in Fort William going back to 1825, and for many years there were two active distilleries in the town. Both Scottish Malt Distillers and Long John Distillers were associated with the area, and today the Ben Nevis Distillery still produces 'The Dew of Ben Nevis', virtually at the foot of the mountain itself. Sadly, the picturesque old Glenlochy Distillery no longer makes whisky, and its traditional, pagoda-shaped still-houses have been emptied of their equipment. Instead, it is run as a guest-house and must have the most distinctive shape of any such establishment in Scotland.

Fort William itself was founded as a garrison town, with the original fort being built by General Monk. Besieged during both the 1715 and 1745 rebellions, Fort William was never captured by the Jacobites and was retained as a garrison for more than another century until it was dismantled in 1855. Relics of this era can still be seen in the West Highland Museum in the town. Fort William was, in 1896, one of the first towns in Britain to have electric light, generated by hydroelectric power, and the town has remained one of the few industrial centres in the Highlands with, as well as whisky-distilling, an aluminium works, the wood-pulp mill at nearby Corpach and a spread of light industry on several estates around the area. Tourism is the other, and now perhaps most important, industry and Fort William is a major regional centre for visitors to the west Highlands.

Just outside the town, on the south bank of the River Lochy, the ruins of the fifteenth-century Inverlochy Castle are in a poor state of preservation. This was originally a massive structure, with circular towers having walls up to 5 m thick. Notable battles were fought here in 1431 and 1645. In the latter, the romantic figure of the great Marquis of Montrose, having led his men in a series of forced marches through the mountains of Lochaber, defeated the forces of the Scottish Covenanters – just one of the dashing exploits which made his name a legend in that period of Scottish history.

GLEN NEVIS IN WINTER

One of the loveliest glens in the western Highlands, and not made any less so by its easy accessibility, Glen Nevis curls for 12 km around the southern and western slopes of Ben Nevis from a starting point on the outskirts of Fort William. A good road can be driven for most of the length of the glen, after which a path leads in less than 2 km to the Steall waterfall which can be spectacular in wet weather. The glen is bounded to the north by the great rounded humps of Ben Nevis and its outliers, Carn Dearg and Meall an Suidhe, and on the other side by the Mamore hills, a chain of fine peaks connected by sweeping ridges. The whole area is a climbers' and walkers' paradise, and the northern end of Scotland's premier long-distance walking route, the West Highland Way, is at the youth hostel in Glen Nevis.

The River Nevis flows down the centre of the glen, placidly in the lower section, precipitously in the upper half where there are spectacular rapids, and a picturesque waterfall – very popular with tourists as it is right by the roadside. Higher still, en route to the Steall waterfall, the river has cut a gorge which would not be out of place in the Himalayas, flanked by towering cliffs on both banks, and where the path at some points must cling to narrow ledges. The bed of the river here is a chaotic jumble of enormous boulders, some as large as houses, beneath which the water disappears for long stretches.

The glen is very popular during the summer months and perhaps some of its tranquillity is lost. In winter, as with most of the Highlands, peace returns as the crowds depart, and in the photograph a quiet backwater of the Nevis, made sluggish by ice, reflects a line of alders outlined in snow. In the background, conifers cover the lower end of a ridge which drops into the valley from one of the Mamore hills.

BEN NEVIS FROM CARN MORE DEARG

On a baking hot day in June, snow patches gleam on the north face of Ben Nevis. As well as being Great Britain's highest mountain at 1340 m (4400 ft) Nevis has the highest mainland cliffs. With little to give scale, it may be hard to appreciate that this enormous rock face approaches 610 m in vertical height, and that the two great ridges in the centre of the picture – North-East Buttress on the left and Tower Ridge – both exceed 670 m in length.

Ben Nevis was first climbed in 1771 by the botanist, James Robertson, on a specimen-gathering expedition. The second recorded ascent, three years later, was by a Welshman, John Williams, on a quest for minerals and gems. He later published a book on mountains in which a geological sketch of Ben Nevis was included. The number of ascents seems to have increased rapidly after this, but most were climbs made in the interests of science; the idea of climbing for pleasure had not yet taken hold and it was to be another fifty years or more before anyone climbed Nevis just for fun. The Ordnance Survey came to the mountain in 1867 and any lingering doubts that Ben Nevis was Britain's highest peak were soon dispelled. Thirteen years later on 1 May 1880, the greatest pioneer of Scottish climbing, William Wilson Naismith, arrived with two friends in Fort William, and the age of climbing had come to Ben Nevis. Not that the relationship between scientific fact-gathering and mountains was over. In fact, far from it – the great Victorian thirst for knowledge was at its height. In October 1883 the Scottish Meteorological Society, having raised £4000 by public subscription, opened an observatory on the summit of Ben Nevis. It was permanently manned by two observers and a cook, and the primary objective was to gather meteorological data, in particular information on Atlantic depressions and the weather systems of the Atlantic seaboard. The observatory was spectacularly successful at this task for the next twenty-one years, though it was never financially secure. The Scottish Meteorological Society could not afford the annual upkeep, and Government help was minimal. In October 1904 the observatory closed, never to reopen. Today the tumbled ruins barely reach shoulder height as the ceaseless winds and arctic conditions on Nevis's summit work slowly but steadily to remove all trace of a remarkable Victorian venture.

CLEARING LOW PRESSURE, LOCH LOCHY

On an early spring morning, the mists and low clouds of what had been a very deep depression over the Western Highlands started to roll away as I drove south after a trip to Skye. An hour earlier, rain had been falling from a grey blanket of cloud which stretched from horizon to horizon, and there seemed little prospect of any change. But such is the extreme variability of Highland weather that, although we had just had three or four days of continuous rain, with a shift of wind to the east, within minutes the clouds were starting to heave and move, and inside half an hour large patches of blue could be seen. The improvement continued steadily and by the time I reached the Great Glen the sun was shining.

Loch Lochy is one of a chain of three freshwater lochs and one sea loch which mark so clearly on any map the line of the Great Glen, the most obvious of Scotland's major geological fault lines. Created by a lateral tear in the earth's crust, the fault was then scoured and deepened by glacial action during successive ice ages, forming the basins in which the lochs lie today. The flanks of the hills ranging along the sides of the Great Glen have been steepened by the same glacial action. They are unsuitable for agriculture, being given over instead to forestry, and the lower slopes of Sron a Choire Ghairbh, the mountain across Loch Lochy, are thickly treed. The Great Glen has been a line of communication since prehistoric times and today one of the main east–west road routes follows the Glen, as well as the Caledonian Canal. The canal was built to enable shipping to avoid the long and perilous passage round the north of Scotland via Cape Wrath and The Pentland Firth, but modern vessels are much too large for its locks, so the canal is now most used by recreational sailors and the occasional fishing boat.

LOCH EILT AND ROIS-BHEINN

The route from Fort William to Mallaig, some 70 km of narrow, twisting, mostly single-carriageway roads through fine coastal and mountain scenery, is one of only two ways to penetrate the still relatively peaceful western extremities of Morvern, Moidart, Ardnamurchan and Morar. Protected and encircled by a ring of sea lochs and mountains, the area is bypassed by the mainstream of both tourism and commerce. The coastline is rough and rocky, and the interior crossed by very few roads. The area is extremely mountainous and, though the hills are not particularly high, they make up for this by their numbers. In 15 km, from where the road leaves the sea at the end of Loch Eil to the western end of Loch Eilt, it passes by no fewer than twelve separate groups of hills over 610 m (2000 ft): many approach 914 m (3000 ft) and a few of the main tops to the north exceed this figure.

The road climbs up through these hills, west of Glenfinnan, only to drop immediately down into the long winding glen which holds Loch Eilt. It is a picturesque place where hill, water and woods combine on an intimate scale. When the picture was taken, a recent fall of snow had brightened the landscape; at ten on a winter's morning, the sun was still not high enough to clear the hills to the east, and only the summits were in direct sunshine. Across the loch, the top of Druim a Fiaclach, just showing above an intervening ridge, was 5 km away. Rois-Bheinn, the highest hill in Moidart and certainly the shapeliest, was almost twice as far. Loch Eilt, partly frozen, held almost perfect reflections of the scene, in water unruffled by even the slightest breeze.

The area has many associations with Prince Charles Edward Stuart ('Bonnie Prince Charlie'). He landed from France in 1745 on the beach of Loch nan Uamh in the Sound of Arisaig, just a few kilometres away, and his standard was raised to call the clans to arms at Glenfinnan, where a monument stands today. After his defeat at Culloden, and months on the run and in hiding, much of it in the surrounding hills, he departed from the same beach a year and two months later, never to return.

River Ailort in Winter

Tree-covered islets such as this, which occur throughout the Highlands, are a testament to two things: that sheep and deer do not like to swim, and that where they can range freely they will reduce the available vegetation to a minimum. In historic times, much of the Highlands of Scotland was tree-covered, with pine, birch and oak being the dominant species. As the population grew and man's intervention in the landscape increased, the trees were progressively cut down for a variety of reasons. Timber was required for building and as fuel; swathes of forest were cut down or burned to prevent outlaws and bandits using them as refuges; ancient Caledonian pines were used for charcoal-burning and iron-smelting; many were felled in retribution after the 1745 rebellion; others were used to build ships for the Napoleonic wars; and yet more, in this century, were made into ammunition boxes. Gradually the landscape assumed the denuded appearance we are familiar with today. In spite of all the depredations of man, some woodland might have regenerated, had it not been for the introduction of sheep. Second only to goats in their destructive capabilities, sheep denude this type of environment of any and all green vegetation and, of course, tender young shoots are especially prized, including those of trees. Red deer also play a part in hindering tree regrowth. Originally woodland animals, the deer ate the bark of trees, lichens and young tree-shoots but the vast Caledonian forest could withstand this. As the forest was reduced, the deer were gradually forced into open country and their diet changed. They still, however, relished the old favourites of bark and tree-shoots, and the remnant woodlands were now vulnerable to both the deer and the huge numbers of sheep that were being introduced. As the forests disappeared, they no longer regenerated. Today the most frequently seen fragments of the ancient forest are on islands, to which sheep and deer do not care to swim; safe from their attentions, the young trees can grow to maturity undisturbed. Luckily, some of the islands are quite large; on the bigger islands of Loch Maree, Loch Morar and Loch Awe you can still walk in woodlands like those of five centuries ago.

Eigg and Rum from near Mallaig

In the aftermath of a westerly spring gale, even after twenty-four hours had passed, there was still enough of a swell running in the Sound of Sleat to require some nimble footwork as waves swept in over the rocky shore, and the sky over the islands gave a strong hint that there was more bad weather to come. Though the entire western seaboard of Scotland is greatly affected by the prevailing Atlantic airstream, and gales can sweep in during any month, some of the coast is given a measure of protection by the islands of the Inner Hebrides. The villages of Mallaig, Morar and Arisaig lie close together within a few kilometres along a glorious length of coast in which rocky headlands alternate with beaches of startling white sand. Where two arms of the sea – the Sound of Sleat and the Sound of Rum – meet, only a narrow stretch of water separates the mainland from the southern end of Skye, Rum and Eigg, and these islands break the worst of the westerly gales and give some relief to the cluster of villages. Any advantage they may gain in this way, however, is offset by another climatic effect of the islands. As warm air, laden with moisture, sweeps in from the Atlantic, it normally passes over any low-lying stretch of coast without dumping this moisture as rain. Here, however, forced to lift up into higher, colder air to pass over the hills of Skye, Rum and Eigg, the clouds condense into rain. Because of this both the islands and the coast off which they lie have one of the wettest climates in Britain.

So often cloud-capped or lost in haze, Rum and Eigg preserve a slight aura of mystery which is helped by the lack of any car ferry service to either island. Any tourists must be prepared to explore on foot, and this disincentive keeps numbers down and the remoter parts of both islands almost unvisited.

MALLAIG AND THE HARBOUR

The little town of Mallaig, in its splendid situation on the shores of the Sound of Sleat in north Morar opposite the Isle of Skye, has a multitude of roles. In spite of its small size – one thousand inhabitants – it is very much the regional centre for this part of the west Highlands, with a large secondary school and a range of shops, hotels and services. It is the end of the romantic 'Road to the Isles', the western terminus of the Fort William railway line, ferry port for southern Skye and the Small Isles, and home base for one of the biggest fishing fleets in western Scotland. Its role as a fishing centre is particularly important and the fishing industry is the major local employer. At the weekend, when the boats are back in port, the harbour bristles with scores of masts of boats both large and small, for there is an inshore fleet which fishes the waters of the Sound of Sleat and along the Morar coast, and a deep-water fleet which fishes both the Minch between Skye and the Outer Hebrides and the Atlantic fishing grounds out towards the remote islands of St Kilda and beyond the Butt of Lewis. The continuing success of local fishing has given rise to one area of controversy. The large fish lorries which take the refrigerated catch away to the south, like all other traffic, must use the very narrow and twisting road which is the only route back through the Morar peninsula towards Fort William. This road is unsuitable for such heavy traffic, but repeated promises by the authorities to upgrade it have not been honoured. In the summer of 1991, local residents blocked the road over a busy holiday weekend to register a protest at the continuing inaction. It remains to be seen whether this will have any effect.

Behind Mallaig, the rocky hill of Carn a'Ghobhair, only 547 m (1790 ft) high, is one of the finest viewpoints in Scotland. On a clear day, the views from its summit take in the length of Loch Nevis, Loch Morar and the wild peaks which surround them, the Isle of Skye and the Cuillins, the distinctive outlines of Rum and Eigg, and the long, low headland of Ardnamurchan, the most westerly point on the British mainland.

The Skye Ferry Leaving Mallaig

Throughout the islands of Western Scotland, and the mainland ports and harbours which communicate with them, there is no escaping the name Caledonian MacBrayne. The ferries sail to all the major islands of the Inner and Outer Hebrides as well as to Bute and Arran in the Firth of Clyde, and the saying 'To the islands by the grace of God and MacBrayne', is as true today as it ever was. Formed from the merger of two very old-established shipping firms – David MacBrayne Ltd and the Caledonian Steam Packet Co. – CalMac, as the company tends to be called, today operates a fleet of modern vessels capable of sailing in most weathers. Recognized as a vital service to the western islands of Scotland, Caledonian MacBrayne receives a certain amount of government subsidy, without which many of the crossings it operates would not be viable.

Ferries like the one in the photograph cross between Mallaig and Armadale on the Sleat peninsula of Skye several times a day in summer. The crossing takes less than half an hour – just enough time for a stroll on deck and a cup of coffee in the restaurant – and makes a pleasant interlude in any journey. As well as for Skye, ferries leave Mallaig for all the small isles: Eigg, Rum, Muck and Canna. These are passenger-only, however, and though the tourist is encouraged to get out and explore the islands, he must do so on foot – a restriction definitely to be applauded in these car-dominated days.

There can be few more romantic journeys in the British Isles than to leave a west-Highland ferry port and sail into a Hebridean sunset. The combination of the sounds of the sea, a few gulls wheeling overhead and a smoky afterglow slowly fading along the western horizon is, and always will be, irresistible – to me, at any rate.

Conifer Forest in Glen Garry

From Invergarry in the Great Glen, a road runs west and north through the heartlands of Glen Shiel and Kintail to Kyle of Lochalsh and the crossing to Skye. In its first few kilometres this road touches the northern shores of Loch Garry, before climbing high above the loch where the whole of its glen lies below like a map. Along this glen, for over 40 km, a narrow road twists and turns the length of Loch Garry, the River Garry and Loch Quoich, climbs through a rocky mountain pass and finally drops down to the sea at Kinloch Hourn, one of the loneliest spots in Britain to be served by a road. At the end of this long and difficult journey there is nothing, not a single house or building of any kind, and the road ends abruptly at a jetty which implies another journey to somewhere more remote, more difficult. There are few places in the Highlands of which I would say this, but Kinloch Hourn has a gloomy feel, even on the sunniest day.

The same is not true of Glen Garry, though this photograph was shot on a moody August day when clouds and rain were always going to win over sunshine. A shift of air opened a window through the mist which had previously obscured everything, and for a moment there was enough brightness to give a sparkle to the waters of the River Garry. In the distance low clouds lifted just enough to show the saddle below Geal Charn, though the tops stayed hidden. The intervening ridges slowly cleared until the nearer tree-tops were etched against further, hazier shapes. Left and right the mist cut off everything else, and for ten minutes or so this view and no other lay below, like a glimpse into another country. There was a deep and windless hush for as long as the vision lasted until, with a barely perceptible change of air, the mist silently drew across again. I waited another hour, but there was no second showing.

EILAN DONAN CASTLE, KINTAIL

One of the best-known of all the Highland castles, Eilan Donan, stands on an island reached by a short causeway in a spectacular setting at the meeting of three fjords – Lochs Duich, Long and Alsh. Archaeological examination has shown that there was an Iron Age fort here, but the present structure is the successor to fortifications first established by King Alexander II of Scotland, in the early part of the thirteenth century, to deter Viking raiders. The original of the present tower was built in the fourteenth century by the Earls of Ross, and later came into the hands of the Mackenzie family, the Earls of Seaforth, and in 1719 figured in a minor Jacobite adventure. The then Earl of Seaforth, who had supported the Jacobite cause in the 1715 rebellion, had been in exile in France and Spain. In 1719 he persuaded the King of Spain into an armed foray in the Scottish Highlands, and sailed from Spain with ten ships and six thousand men. A stormy sea-passage took a heavy toll, however, and Seaforth arrived in the Outer Hebrides with only a small fraction of his force still intact. He raised a few hundred men in the islands and proceeded to his stronghold at Eilan Donan in Kintail, but when he was wounded in the subsequent battles with Government forces, the heart went out of his troops and the rebellion fizzled out. During the affair, while garrisoned by Seaforth's Spanish troops, Eilan Donan was bombarded by three English frigates and almost completely destroyed. It was to remain a ruin for the next two hundred years until it was restored between 1912 and 1930 by a descendant of the Macrae family, former custodians of the castle under the Earl of Seaforth. Some parts of the tower and an unusual hexagonal stone water-tank remained, but the walls of all the surrounding buildings had been reduced to stumps. The restoration was carried out using old engravings as guides so that, although the present exterior is almost all modern, it is quite faithful to the original appearance. The castle now operates as a museum, showing Macrae, Mackenzie and Jacobite relics.

THE SKYE FERRY AT KYLE OF LOCHALSH

In summer, three different crossings to Skye are serviced by ferries: the long crossing from Mallaig to Armadale at the south end of the island; the shortest of the three across the narrows between remote Glenelg and the equally remote Kylerhea on the eastern tip of the island; and this, the most popular, which makes the five minute crossing from Kyle of Lochalsh on the mainland to Kyleakin on Skye. There have been repeated promises that a bridge would be built here, since the volume of traffic in summer is heavy and at busy times the ferry queues can stretch for miles. This is obviously a great inconvenience to everyone, especially local inhabitants and tradespeople, and pressure from the latter eventually led to a commitment to build the bridge. However, economic times being what they are, the promise may have lapsed, and it was very noticeable, in the summer of 1991 that two large new ferries had appeared on the service between Kyle and Kyleakin. From the visitor's point of view the ferry is infinitely preferable, even if there are occasional queues. A sea-crossing, however short, always has an exotic feel and causes just enough interruption to the journey to make you realize that something different is happening – you really are on the way to an island. To drive unhindered across a bridge would hardly be the same thing and it is hard to imagine what kind of structure could be in keeping with the magnificence of the surroundings. A sympathetic architectural solution is not impossible, but when holding costs down is the most important factor, as it probably will be, the result may not be as aesthetically pleasing as it might be. For now, however, there seems no immediate danger of an enormous bridge blighting this particular land- and sea-scape; the ferries will roll for a time yet.

ABANDONED JETTY, LOCH KISHORN

In the early 1970s, after much lobbying for and against, and in the face of competition from other possible locations, Loch Kishorn was chosen as a site for oil-rig construction. Its main advantage was a sheltered, deep-water anchorage into which construction materials could be shipped, and where the huge exploration rigs could be floated after construction. On the north shore of the loch at the foot of the Applecross Pass, a vast area was cleared and levelled, and the construction yard, the size of a small airfield, built out into the water, with all the necessary jetties and moorings. For a few years in the 1970s it was boom time and, like a gold-rush town, constructors' offices and accommodation mushroomed – b&bs and hotels were full of oil-rig people for miles around. But with the 1980s came the doldrums: oil exploration went into recession and orders for rigs dried up. When a revival happened later in the decade, foreign yards had developed cheaper methods of rig manufacture, and British yards were no longer competitive – work dried up. No doubt the present owner of the yard would not accept that it has been abandoned, but it is hard to deny the evidence of one's eyes. All of the buildings have gone and the vast yard lies empty, apart from the detritus of scrap metal and builders' rubbish which litters it. Offshore the piers moulder away untended, and in a tiny corner of the yard the only activity in May 1992 was a couple of scrap-metal merchants dismantling the last visible structure. The yard sits like some ugly excrescence, disfiguring, probably for ever, the face of the once beautiful Loch Kishorn. It is a memorial to ill-conceived, ill-planned and uncontrolled development which had nothing to do with the long-term prosperity of the region – a familiar story in the Scottish Highlands.

BEALACH NA BA – THE APPLECROSS PASS

The name means 'the pass of the cattle' and the first road here was a drove road, down which cattle raised on the Applecross peninsula started their journey to the markets of the south. It is the most spectacular road in the Highlands, climbing from sea-level along the shores of Loch Kishorn to 625 m (2050 ft) in just 3 km, first in a long straight haul up the glen between two dramatically steep but flat-topped mountains, Meall Gorm and Sgurr a Chaorochain, then spiralling through a series of tight hairpins to a final pull up to the pass. The views are wild and inspiring, and the weather at the summit car park on a summer's day can be anything from a windless heatwave to a raging gale complete with snow or hail. Easy walks lead from the top of the pass along the relatively flat summit plateaus of the flanking hills to even more stunning views from the cliff-tops.

Once over the pass, the road leads more easily down, westwards, to the village of Applecross. This has a single row of houses facing the sea, a tiny hotel, a single shop and a very antiquated petrol pump. A string of even smaller hamlets straggles south for 4 km down the coast to Toscaig, where a harbour gave sea access before the road was built. In Gaelic, Applecross was called A Chromraich 'The Sanctuary' – in memory of the community founded here by St Maelrubha in the seventh century. He was another early Irish Christian missionary, more or less contemporary with St Columba. The monastery became one of the foremost centres of Christianity in Scotland at that time; only Iona was more important. It was sacked by the Vikings around AD 720. St Maelrubha was killed by the Vikings, not here at Applecross but while on a mission to the far north, at Skaill in Sutherland.

SHIELDAIG, WEST INVERNESS-SHIRE

Like many Highland place-names it is Norse – Sildvik – and means 'Bay of Herrings'. The herring are long gone from these waters, but the bay still holds one relic of the past – an island entirely covered in Scots pine. Originally a crofting and fishing community, the village now depends quite heavily on tourism and most of the old way of life has gone, as in many small places in the west Highlands. Shieldaig is very prettily situated on its bay near the mouth of Loch Torridon, and its proximity to the magnificent mountain ranges of Torridon, as well as Applecross and the Beinn Damh hills, attracts hill-walkers and makes tourism a year-round industry. A walker's track goes west from the village to follow the coast all the way to Applecross, giving fine views across the Inner Sound to the islands of Raasay and Skye, while inland the miniature summit of Ben Shieldaig, just 500 m (1640 ft) high, gives an uninterrupted panorama of all the surrounding ranges.

Near the village the National Nature Reserve of Rassal covers an area of more than 80 hectares and includes a large natural ash-wood, one of the very few anywhere in Scotland and the most northerly in Britain. The trees grow on an undulating limestone pavement, and the area is particularly rich in mosses which in early summer are dotted with yellow primroses and purple orchids. The woods have been enclosed to give some protection from grazing animals and to allow regeneration, and the reserve has become a sanctuary for many species of bird whose normal habitat is broad-leaved woodlands, and which are therefore quite rare in many parts of the Highlands. Insect and animal life also abounds, and the reserve is an oasis of green in a landscape otherwise characterized by rather barren sandstone mountains and peat moorland.

LOCH MAREE, WESTER ROSS

This long, freshwater loch stretches some 20 km from Poolewe on the west coast to Kinlochewe deep in the interior, with Slioch, one of Scotland's boldest peaks, on its northern shores. The name may have come from St Maree (St Maelrubha) who founded the monastery at Applecross and who is reputed to have spent some time as a hermit on one of the larger islands here in the loch. Local legend has it that he is buried on the island, but this claim is contested by more than one other location.

Loch Maree and its surroundings are classic west Highland territory, with high mountains, oak-woods, pine forest, sparkling water and tree-clad islands. Here, too, a National Nature Reserve has been set up to give some protection to both plant and animal species. The area is very rich in wildlife, again the classic species of the Highlands: red deer and roe deer, wild cat and pine marten, badger and fox. Eagles, falcons and buzzards patrol the skies, while in the waters of the loch there are greylag geese and black-throated divers. Salmon and sea-trout penetrate up the River Ewe. On the south-facing shores of the loch there are fine natural oak-woods which support a wide range of other plants and animals, while the north-facing shores have one of the best remaining Scots-pine forests and one of the few that is regenerating adequately to ensure its survival.

The climate is wet and, for the most part, mild. At nearby Inverewe, more than a hundred years ago, Osgood Mackenzie created a garden which has since become famous. Tended and extended by his family, it has been National Trust property since 1952. It boasts rhododendrons, azaleas, lilies and sub-tropical plants from South America, Africa and the Himalayas.

FERRY TERMINAL AT ARMADALE, SKYE

The pier at Armadale on the Sleat peninsula in southern Skye is just another in the network of little ports and harbours, throughout the islands and the Scottish west coast, that the ubiquitous ferry company, Caledonian MacBrayne, makes use of. Car ferries run from here to Mallaig, on the mainland, during spring and summer, and the crossing is used by thousands of visitors annually. Demoted during the winter months to be a passenger ferry only, the link is still vital to the local populations on both sides of the crossing, where bus services are timed to the ferry movements.

Mallaig lies about 9 km to the south-east, across the waters of the Sound of Sleat. Along the coast north of Mallaig stretches one of the loneliest parts of the Highlands, whose hills form the backdrop to the pier. No road penetrates the mountain fastness of Knoydart, a peninsula whose roots stretch some 55 km back to the Great Glen, bounded north and south by Lochs Garry, Quoich and Arkaig and by the great fjords of Loch Hourn and Loch Nevis. Accessible only on foot or by boat, Knoydart nevertheless has settlements, the main one being Inverie, and there is some crofting, deer-stalking and forestry. In the centre of the photograph, Ladhar Beinn, the most westerly of all mainland ' Monroes' (hills above 914 m (3000 ft)), and the highest in Knoydart proper, rises clear of its neighbours with a profile visible all the way down the south-east coast of Skye. The old name for Knoydart was 'the Rough Bounds', and with good reason; riven by deep glens between steep-sided mountains and crossed by fast-flowing rivers, the almost trackless interior is difficult for even hardened walkers. It was yet another of the remote, isolated regions where Prince Charles Edward Stuart sought refuge in 1745 after the tragedy of Culloden.

SEA CLIFFS AT BRAES, SKYE

On a moody, overcast day, sheep grazed the grassy cliffs of Gedintailor at Braes on the east coast of Skye. To the north, Ben Tianavaig and the houses of Camustianavaig, tiny at this distance, lay beneath lowering skies. Braes is famous in the recent annals of the Highlands as it was here, in 1882, that crofters who had been evicted from elsewhere in Skye and Raasay fought a pitched battle with police and soldiers sent from Glasgow. These had been sent to arrest the crofters as dissidents and unruly elements, and in the aftermath of the battle some did indeed end up in prison. But as the ripples caused by the affair spread wider, it was not long before the then Prime Minister, William Gladstone, a Scot related to a former owner of nearby Raasay island, reacted positively. A Royal Commission was set up under Lord Napier, whose brief was to examine and report on the situation in the Scottish Highlands, and though landowners and their agents would have their say, the ordinary people of the Highlands were to have a voice for the first time. The Battle of Braes had not been an isolated incident, though perhaps the most large-scale and violent of these events. Scattered around the Highlands there had been skirmishes between starving evictees and the authorities, and in some cases the crofters had forcibly repossessed parts of their former lands. Now real help was at hand. In 1886 the Crofters Act was passed, giving them security of tenure and preventing their eviction. It was too late for the hundreds of thousands who had been forced overseas and the Highland population continued to decline, but it was something, and at least those who remained could work the land as they always had.

Braes is also known as the home of the distinguished Gaelic poet, Sorley Maclean, who was born and brought up at Oskaig in Raasay and whose forebears had themselves been evicted from Hallaig, in Raasay. Sadly for most people, Sorley Maclean's output has been almost exclusively in Gaelic, for his work has been favourably compared to many leading poets of the twentieth century; parallels have been drawn, in particular, with T.S. Eliot. A collection of Maclean's poems, published in 1943, has been described as a landmark in Scottish literary history. More recently, some of his own English translations have appeared, so that we now have an opportunity to enjoy the work of this leading Gaelic artist.

THE QUIRANG, STAFFIN, SKYE

The actual rock feature in the photograph is called the Needle, for obvious reasons, and is only one, though possibly the most extravagant, of the amazing collection of cliffs, pinnacles and towers known collectively as The Quirang, near Staffin in Trotternish, the great north-eastern arm of Skye. The Quirang itself (whose name means 'pillared enclosure') is just the northern end of a long scarp of cliffs that runs almost unbroken from Portree, capital of Skye, to Staffin, 32 km away. Unmistakable from the main coast road, this line of cliffs rarely falls below 300 m (980 ft) and, as well as the Quirang as its northern termination, has an equally fantastic mountain called The Storr at its southern end. Its most famous feature is called The Old Man of Storr – a basalt pillar some 50 m (160 ft) high, standing in a group of a dozen or so shorter, weird-shaped pinnacles. Both the Needle of The Quirang and The Old Man have been climbed, the latter by Don Whillans in 1955.

The Quirang and The Storr were created by land-slippage in pre-historic times, when the soft bedrock below the thick layer of the volcanic basalt which forms much of northern Skye became incapable of bearing the weight. In both cases a fascinating jumble of rock features has resulted. In the case of The Quirang, many of these have been named, such as The Needle, The Prison and The Table. Shinty is supposed to have been played on The Table, a flat area of grass high on the cliffs. These hills and cliffs are also of great interest to geologists, with the effects of rotational land-slippage, step faults and glacial action all visible within a very small area.

Duirinish Churchyard, Skye

Nearby Dunvegan Castle is the only stately home on Skye and the home of Clan Macleod of Skye. Its pebble-dashed Victorian exterior, however, does not make it the most photogenic castle in Scotland. Outside the village of Dunvegan, the little churchyard of Duirinish looks across the land-locked waters of inner Loch Dunvegan to two impressive flat-topped hills – Macleod's Tables. Their proper names are Healaval Mhor and Healaval Bheag – the Big and Small Flagstone Fell, respectively – and they were formed from layers of basalt by a horizontal flow of lava during the volcanic era on Skye. As the surrounding landscape eroded away, the Tables, composed of harder material, were left standing clear.

The popular name 'Macleod's Tables' derives from a legend, one version of which has it that a sixteenth-century chief of Clan Macleod, who was being entertained to dinner in baronial splendour somewhere in the south, boasted that he had an even finer dinner table. On being given an opportunity to return the hospitality, at dusk Macleod took his guest on horseback to the summit of Healaval Mhor where they dined, surrounded by hundreds of clan retainers carrying flaming torches, beneath a ceiling of stars, on a tabletop of flat turf some acres in extent. It is certainly a nice story. It seems more probable, if less entertaining, that the shape of the hills recalled a flat tabletop and, since they were part of the Macleod lands, they were dubbed with the name.

The hill in the photograph is Healaval Bheag – named as the smaller of the two, but actually the higher. The Vikings who first named them must have approached from the north down Loch Dunvegan, when the lower of the two hills, being nearer, would have appeared higher; thus they got the names the wrong way round.

BLA BHEINN AND CLACH GLAS FROM TORRIN, SKYE

The mountains of southern Skye are divided into two named groups, according to their appearance – the Red and the Black Cuillin. Both of these are then subdivided geographically, with the Red Cuillin, which are rounded granite hills, forming separate groups east and west of Strath Mor. Distanced from the main Black Cuillin ridge by the yawning gulf of Glen Sligachan, Bla Bheinn ('Blue Mountain') and its near neighbour, Clach Glas ('Grey Rock'), form a distinct mountain range, but one which geologically is still part of the Black Cuillin, so called because of the coloration of the rocks – gabbro and basalt – of which they are constructed.

Seen across Loch Slapin, Bla Bheinn and Clach Glas present a stunning panorama of mountain, sea and sky, hard to better anywhere in the Highlands. Torrin is the home of white Skye marble, which is quarried only a few hundred metres away. Nearby beaches have been bleached by marble dust, washed out of the quarry, and at high tide the waters of the loch gleam an irridescent green as sunlight reflects from the pure white seabed. An unseasonal snow fall had highlighted the upper rocks of the mountains when the photograph was taken. (A few days earlier I had arrived in Skye at the beginning of June, for a few days climbing, to find the main Cuillin ridge in almost full winter conditions.)

The area has had its day of controversy. Some years ago, the army, without consultation with the local authorities or conservation groups, decided to build a Land Rover track across the moor around the southern end of Bla Bheinn, and on into Coire'uisg below the main Cuillin ridge, to ease the problem of mountain rescue. The existing footpath had previously been found quite sufficient, and the ugly scar caused by the new road raised many objections. However, the unmaintained track soon began to revert to its former state; bridges were washed away, and vegetation is reclaiming the raw verges and erosion damage.

Bla Bheinn has one of the few summits in the Black Cuillin which can be reached without the need for some elementary rock-climbing, and even here the traverse between its two tops is more than just a walk. But the south ridge which runs easily down to Camasunary is a mere stroll, and gives views of the main ridge and the seascape of Rum and the Small Isles, unrivalled anywhere.

Gars-Bheinn from Elgol, Skye

The most southerly of the Cuillin hills, Gars-Bheinn looks straight down on the waters of Loch Scavaig, another of the sea lochs on Skye's deeply indented west coast, and across to the scattered crofting and fishing community of Elgol, 7 km away. Elgol, at the end of the Strathaird peninsula which thrusts out into the sea between Loch Scavaig and Loch Slapin, can barely be called a village, though it boasts a shop and post office, and a fine little school down near its fishing jetty. It is a scattered community – 'townships' are what they tend to be called in the islands – whose crofters are favoured by a stretch of fertile pasture, which has formed because of an island of limestone-based soil amid an ocean of sour peat-bog. From the top of the hamlet there are broad views across Loch Scavaig to both the Cuillin hills and the Island of Soay tucked below them; at a greater distance to the west, Canna, Rum and Eigg lie along the horizon; heading north along the shore, a rough track leads to Loch Coruisk and the Cuillin.

It may sometimes seem that there are few places in the west Highlands that do not claim some connection with Prince Charles Edward Stuart, and Elgol is no exception. However, it has more justification than many. Still on the run from the Redcoats, he landed at Elgol disguised as a servant, Lewis Caw, and was warmly received by the Mackinnons of Skye who were loyal to the Jacobite cause. They feasted him in a cave on the seashore to the south of the village, now, of course, called Princes Charles's Cave. From Elgol he made his way to the mainland and finally to permanent exile in France.

SGURR NAN GILLEAN, CUILLIN HILLS, SKYE

Not quite the highest of the Cuillin, Sgurr nan Gillean would certainly take many votes as the most shapely. When seen from Sligachan on the road to Portree, the mountain has all the drama of a Gothic cathedral, and during the approach on foot its northern ridge looms above the walker with a fierce array of rock gendarmes, deep-cut notches and towers, which earn for it the name Pinnacle Ridge. Traditionally, Sgurr nan Gillean has been taken to mean 'the peak of the young men', but the word Gillean may come from the Norse 'gil', meaning gully. 'The Peak of The Gullies' would not be thought an inappropriate name by anyone who had stood below the deep gashes of Pinnacle Ridge. Sgurr nan Gillean is the first main peak on the Cuillin ridge for anyone attempting the complete north–south traverse, and, properly, should be climbed via the pinnacles, an outing that requires rock-climbing experience and equipment. From its summit, the black and shattered gabbro falls dizzyingly away into the depths of Harta Coire and Coir'uisg – 'the coire of the waters' – where a complex of streams drain into Loch Coruisk in one of the most dramatic of all British landscapes.

Tourists, since Boswell and Johnson, have been making the pilgrimage to view the Cuillin from Coruisk and, since travel into the Highlands was popularized during the Victorian era, the Cuillin has been a Mecca for climbers. The crest of the main ridge curves for a spectacular 12 km around Coir'uisg, never dropping below 760 m (2490 ft) and with fourteen summits over 914 m (3000 ft). The rock architecture is unrivalled in Britain, and in winter the main traverse is the equal of a serious Alpine expedition. The photograph was shot from Sgurr a Bhasteir – 'Executioner's Peak' – on an evening in June when the remnants of a late fall of snow made abstract patterns across the sweep of black gabbro below the peaks.

LOCH BRITTLE, SKYE

Around the northern foot of the Cuillin Hills, a deep and lovely glen winds down to the sea. This is Glen Brittle, launching pad for ten thousand climbing expeditions into the Cuillin, and beloved of mountaineers and tourists alike. It meets the sea as a dramatic fjord about 5 km long, whose rocky flanks, though not very high, fall steeply to the water. The coastline of Skye, especially in the west and north, is etched all the way round with similar sea lochs, many of which penetrate far inland. On the beach at the landward end of Loch Brittle, black sand gives a straightforward clue to the volcanic origins of the surrounding hills and mountains, but, like most of the western Highlands, the landforms owe their present-day shapes largely to the action of glaciers during the most recent ice ages. Glen Brittle was scooped out by a west-running glacier. Later, as the climate warmed, the melting ice caps all over northern Europe caused sea-levels to rise, and the trench left in this glen when the glacier retreated was filled by the advancing sea. Repeated many times along western and northern seaboards, this process created not only Scotland's deeply indented coast but also the fjords of Norway.

When the photograph was taken at 10.30 p.m. on an evening in early June, the sun had just sunk beneath the hills of Geodha Daraich – the headland on the north side of Loch Brittle – and the afterglow was to last another two hours. A Hebridean sunset like this, in the calm of a midsummer evening, with the sky a deep gold along the horizon, flaming red through the streamers of cloud and fading overhead to deepest midnight blue, is a sight that stays in the memory for a very long time.

THE CUILLIN OF RUM

Considerable debate surrounds the spelling of both names (though I am assured that these are the correct versions, in spite of Ordnance Survey usage), both of which derive from old Norse and mean 'the high rocky peaks of the wide island'. This is an apt enough description of the island's fine chain of mountains when seen from the sea, which is the first view the Vikings would have had. Like their more famous namesakes, the Cuillin of Skye, they are constructed mainly of gabbro, that roughest and most climbable of rocks. The individual names of the mountains are also Norse – from the left: Askival, the spear-shaped peak; Traillval, the troll's peak; and Ainshval, the peak of the ridge. The highest is Askival, which rises to 812 m (2660 ft) and whose summit is a mere 2.5 km from the sea which lies beyond the hills in this view.

The photograph was taken from Harris Glen, a beautiful but deserted valley which runs from the heart of the island to the fertile oasis of Harris on the island's southwest coast. As in so much of the Highlands, Rum's mountains look down on a landscape empty of people and with hardly any trace of their former presence. Rum has the unenviable distinction of being the only island which was *entirely* cleared of people – the last two hundred were put on a boat for Nova Scotia in 1828 by the laird, Maclean of Coll. The background to the migration was the usual one: first the glens were cleared of crofts to make way for sheep, and the people moved to the coasts; then it was discovered that the people could not make a living by fishing. But the real origin of the miseries of Rum's people lay in the greed of their own clan chiefs, hungry for luxury.

Today the island is a nature reserve, administered by Scottish Natural Heritage, and its small population consists entirely of their specialists, support staff and their families. Notable and important wildlife studies are carried out on the island, and a project to reintroduce the sea eagle to Scotland's wilder coasts originated on Rum, with some success. People, however, are still barely welcome on the island – large tracts of it are out of bounds and permission must be sought in advance to climb any of the hills or to camp for a night. This is a sad hangover from Rum's sadder past and, though, of course, it is important that the wildlife can exist and be studied undisturbed, the virtual exclusion of people from this stunningly beautiful island makes it a lonely place.

KINLOCH CASTLE, ISLE OF RUM

Built at the turn of the century by the Bullough family – mine owners, engineers and inventors – Kinloch Castle's brash Edwardian exterior conceals an interior of greater charm, and some novelty. Relinquished by the last remnants of the family in the 1940s, the castle, like the island, is administered by Scottish Natural Heritage and has been run for some years as a hotel. Though most of the really valuable objects have been removed to the Scottish Museum of Antiquities, the house is still a relative treasure trove of period furniture and fascinating artefacts. As well as being inventors, the Bulloughs were travellers of note, with their own ocean-going steam yacht carrying a retinue that included a photographer – a ground-floor room in the house is lined with leather-bound volumes of the original prints that he produced during their voyages to the Americas, Europe and the Far East. On the balcony of the Great Hall, a pair of matching Chinese porcelain jars, about 2 m tall, was reputedly too valuable to be risked on the perilous journey – via tractor-and-trailer and fishing boat – to the mainland and the museum. The house boasts an early form of central heating, and the bedrooms still have their original 90-year-old baths with shower and jacuzzi as built-in features. Entertainment was provided by music from the orchestral organ, powered by compressed air and playing automatically, pianola-style.

Though it was intended as the ultimate in romantic hideaways, the Bulloughs never used the house much. The inventor's beautiful French wife hated the wet west-Highland weather and the midges which plagued the island throughout late summer and autumn. In that respect, at least, the island is still the same today.

NORTHERN RAASAY FROM DUN CAAN

Raasay is a beautiful island of the inner Hebrides, lying only some 10 km from the west coast of Inverness-shire, and sheltered from the prevailing westerlies by the great bulk of Skye. It has a sad history. Though never densely populated, today it is an island of very few people, as the photograph shows, and yet another part of the Highlands that never recovered from the Clearances. In Raasay's case, however, the island's downfall began earlier, with the aftermath of the 1745 rebellion when Prince Charles Edward Stuart was given sanctuary by the the ruling family on Raasay, the MacLeods. Their downfall resulted in the terrorizing and pillaging of the island by Hanoverian troops and supporters. Though the family was restored in the amnesty of 1747 and did their best for the islanders for a time, the people never really recovered. The first recorded emigration began in 1803, and by the 1830s the glens were being cleared of people and the empty lands leased out to sheep farmers from the south. When the Macleod family finally went bankrupt and had to emigrate themselves, the island was sold at auction to the first of a long line of owners who were 'non-native'. Though some of these adopted relatively enlightened attitudes to the plight of the islanders, essentially their main interest in the island was pecuniary, and when it suited them they did not hesitate from further clearances, or from selling the island on at a profit. At various times other calamities occurred: the kelp industry – the gathering and processing of seaweed for use elsewhere in the manufacture of glass and soap – collapsed; there was a succession of harvest failures; potato blight destroyed entire crops; and when in the late 1870s the then owner began to clear even sheep from the island – in favour of deer, grouse and rabbits for a sporting estate – the native people were seen as even more superfluous.

Nor did the advent of the twentieth century see an end to the continuing depopulation of the island, though in 1922 the Raasay Estate was bought by the Scottish Board of Agriculture in an effort to give those islanders who remained some security. However, there was yet to follow another episode of bizarre and protracted absentee ownership which has today left Raasay with a population of just one hundred and fifty, many of whom are elderly or summer visitors only.

RAASAY HOUSE, CLACHAN BAY

Originally built by the MacLeod family, then rebuilt after the 1745 rebellion, Raasay House was visited by Johnson and Boswell in 1773. The island, the house and the Macleod family all seem to have delighted Boswell, who described the laird, Captain Malcolm MacLeod, as 'a father to his people'. For nearly the next two centuries the house, either enlarged and looked after or abandoned and neglected by its various owners, played little direct role in the island's history, save possibly for one episode. Above the little private harbour in Clachan Bay, an elaborate stone wall runs in a semicircle between the grounds of the house and the sea. At each end the wall is embellished with a carved stone mermaid, of at least 'life' size. These were sculpted in Italy, and transported at vast expense to Raasay, where it is said they were the ultimate factor in the Macleod family's bankruptcy in 1843.

The modern history of the house begins in 1960 when it was sold by the Scottish Department of Agriculture to a Sussex pathologist, Dr Green. Over a period of about seven years, and for less than £8000, Dr Green was to buy the mansion and grounds, various other buildings, the harbour, home farm, Borodale House, the boathouse and the estate cottages. Over the eighteen years of his ownership he visited the island only once, while his property was allowed to fall into disuse and neglect. Houses and cottages were left untenanted, and Raasay House itself became a shambles, empty and vandalized, its valuables stolen and dispersed. At the same time, Dr Green obstructed and delayed every attempt at development on the island. The most notorious episode was that of his blocking the provision of a car ferry to the island, by a refusal to sell or allow the upgrading of the pier at Clachan where the local authority intended the ferry to dock. When the matter was finally decided by compulsory purchase after several years of wrangling, it proved to be the end of any pretence at interest in the island on the part of Dr Green. His latter years as owner, up until 1979, were characterized by utter neglect, though like many other landlords of Raasay before him, his last act was to sell the island at a very handsome profit, in this case to the Highlands and Islands Development Board.

THE TORRIDON HILLS FROM LIATHACH

Few climbers would dispute a claim that the Torridon group of mountains is the finest in the northern Highlands, and many would argue that it is the grandest in all of Scotland. The hills range along Upper Loch Torridon and both sides of Glen Torridon, though the best-known and finest of them – Beinn Alligin, Liathach and Beinn Eighe – lie on the north side of the valley. Of the three, only Beinn Alligin is lower than 1000 m (3280 ft) and, rising as they do from sea-level, their great eastern cliffs of weathered sandstone are deeply impressive, with Liathach especially soaring above the road in Glen Torridon. All three are more mountain ranges than simple mountains; Alligin has four summits, Liathach seven and Beinn Eighe eight. Many of these tops are capped with white quartzite which gleams in the sun and can be mistaken for snow.

In this view from near the highest summit of Liathach, Beinn Alligin, Beinn Dearg and Baosbheinn lie across the great gulf of Coire Mhic Nobuil. In the far distance the north Atlantic gleams dully where it bites deeply into the land at Gair Loch. No road crosses this great swathe of territory and all settlements are confined to the periphery. In the whole of a vast area of nearly 500 sq km – bounded by Glen Torridon to the south, Loch Maree to the north and the Atlantic coast in the west – there is no permanent human presence. The Torridon ranges form a superb mountain wilderness whose unique qualities have long been prized by walkers and climbers, and though much of it is in private hands and is managed as typical Highland sporting estates, access to the hills remains unrestricted for most of the year. The importance of the region to the national heritage has also been recognized, and an area enclosing Beinn Alligin, Liathach and much of Beinn Dearg and Beinn Eighe is owned by the National Trust for Scotland, guaranteeing public access to these hills at all times and in perpetuity.

SHORE STREET, ULLAPOOL, FROM THE PIER

Like many other villages round the coastline of the Highlands, Ullapool is of relatively recent origin having been founded in the late 1780s by the British Fisheries Society. At that time the Highland clearances were in full swing and the inhabitants were being removed wholesale from the interiors of the great estates, formerly clan lands, to make way for sheep-farming on an industrial scale. Most were forced to emigrate, mainly to the USA and Canada, but some stayed on and tried to eke out a living along the coast. Fishing was seen as an appropriate way for them to earn a means of survival. Fishing villages were established, sometimes sponsored by the lairds carrying out the evictions, sometimes, as here, by benevolent societies.

Ullapool is still a busy fishing port and in recent years has grown rapidly. It acquired more importance as a communication and transport centre with the establishment, about ten years ago, of a vehicle ferry service to Stornoway in the Outer Hebrides. Tourism had already played a major part in the local economy for many years, and the new ferry confirmed Ullapool as the major touring centre in Wester Ross. It is still tiny, however, with under a thousand inhabitants, and at the quieter times of year including early Spring when this picture was taken, has a sleepy charm all of its own. There is spectacular mountain and coastal scenery all around and wildlife and fishing are major local attractions. In recent years, huge east European fishing fleets based themselves in Loch Broom, the fjord in which Ullapool sits, and made one of the major sights of the region – the loch filled from end to end with scores of huge deep-sea fishing vessels ('Klondykers') and even more massive factory vessels. Russian, Polish and Czech were more common in the streets of Ullapool than Gaelic, and it was not unknown for sailors from the fleet to marry and settle down locally. But over-fishing depleted the Atlantic fishing stocks and now the fleets are gone – only a few lone trawlers dot the waters of Loch Broom.

Tanera More and the Assynt Hills

Just a few kilometres offshore from the Coigeach peninsula in Wester Ross, Tanera More is the largest of the charming archipelago known collectively as the Summer Isles. The only island under year-round occupation, Tanera More supports crofting, fishing and fish-farming, as well as a religious foundation which began the regeneration of the island by refurbishing several of the original cottages. In summer, visitors are drawn by the remote landscapes, abundant wildlife including breeding seal colonies and sea-fishing. Happily, the number of tourists actually making landfall on the islands is controlled by the restricted transport to and from the mainland and by the relative scarcity of holiday accommodation. It is to be hoped that nothing will drastically alter this situation and that the islands will remain in their unspoilt condition, a sanctuary both for the wildlife and the few inhabitants.

About 3 km away across Badentarbat Bay, the village of Achiltibuie straggles along above the shore on the south-western edge of a rough heather moorland punctuated by deep freshwater lochs. Above the moor the hills of Coigach and Assynt rise, each in isolated splendour. None of these hills is particularly high, but their form and situation give them a curious grandeur. On a day of low swirling cloud, not infrequent anywhere in the Highlands, they can suddenly appear, shouldering the mists aside like primeval beasts. Here, Suilven, Canisp, Stac Polly and Cul Mor are ranged along the northern horizon on what was a late August day of sunshine and sharp ice-cold showers, as the strong prevailing westerly whisked Atlantic rain clouds rapidly overhead.

The Anchorage, Tanera More

Lying close to shore but still proper islands, the larger of the Summer Isles have that delicious sense of really being away from it all. Though it may take just a few minutes on the fast little ferry to come across from the jetty below Badentarbat, once the boat has turned around and headed off back to the mainland, a wonderful feeling of remoteness comes flooding in. Somehow this is accentuated by the proximity of the hills and houses of Polbain, just across the narrow channel north of Baden Bay – so near but, when the ferry has gone, so far. There are ways of visiting Tanera More and its smaller, uninhabited partner, Tanera Beg, without the need to spend a night on the island: cruise operators from Ullapool land on Tanera More, giving people just enough time for a short stroll ashore. A similar trip runs to Tanera Beg, where visitors go mainly for a brief look at the wildlife. But that's hardly the way to experience gems like the Summer Isles; much better to watch the ferry disappear off back to Badentarbat, and spend a couple of days walking the island's heathery little hills and rocky shores. There is bed and breakfast to be had in summer, and a wealth of sheltered spots to camp in. There may not much in the way of shopping, but the tea-shop opens when the cruise-boats come in! Tanera More is only 3 km from north to south, and 2 km from east to west, so you can easily walk round it in a day, and it well repays such an investment of time.

Towards the northern end of the island, three tiny lochs nestle among the heather and sweet-smelling dwarf juniper, and from the lonely west coast a raft of smaller islands and skerries streams out towards the horizon. Even on a calm day a ceaseless Atlantic swell runs through the narrow channels that separate the islands, and on any day when a wind has raised the height of the waves the spray can be spectacular. Tanera More is home to nearly fifty breeding species of birds, and the air is usually full of their cries. Seals also come and go in the surrounding waters. For a couple of days, if the weather holds, this can be paradise. For those who live here all year round, fishing and tending the fish-farms, it probably doesn't always seem like that, but for every hardship there are the compensations of living in such a beautiful environment, thus it seems unlikely that the Summer Isles will ever be deserted.

SUNSET OVER ISLE RISTOL

Isle Ristol, like Horse Island to the south and Priest Island to the west, is separated a little from the main group of the Summer Isles and is the closest inshore of all these islands. At low tide, just a short causeway separates this small, uninhabited island from the mainland. The sheltered water created by the island on both sides of the causeway is used as an anchorage by all sorts of sailors. Local fishermen predominate but, in the summer months, many yachts come in to provision in the shops at Polbain and Achiltibuie, or to ride out a westerly gale in the lee of the island. Isle Ristol is only 0.5 km long and almost entirely covered in heather, which provides grazing for a few sheep. When the tide is right, a few people may cross to the island to enjoy its splendid and totally unspoilt beaches, otherwise it is without people. Other outliers of the Summer Isles group, like Horse and Priest Islands, are even more rarely visited because of their greater remoteness, especially Priest Island and the nearby islet of Glas Leac Beag. The one type of human visitor that does occasionally find a way to these islands is the bird-watcher. Uninhabited and far from human activity, the islands are a haven for bird life, and many species of seabird and migrants breed or make feeding stops there. Glas Leac Beag has long been the site for a large colony of black-backed gulls, and their guano has caused a major shift in the island's ecology. Instead of being rather acidic and heather-covered, Glas Leac Beag's soil is fertile and supports a rich growth of grass which turns the island a brilliant green during all the warmer months of the year. As a result, about three hundred barnacle geese graze there during the winter and the entire local population of greylags spend the summer there.

STAC POLLY, INVERPOLLY NATIONAL NATURE RESERVE

'A mountain in miniature', – Stac Polly (Stac Pollaidh) rises abruptly from the moors above the sinuous waters of Loch Lurgainn on the borders of Assynt and Coigach in Wester Ross. With a shape that might be more appropriate to Nevada and its buttes, Stac Polly is a monument in weathered Torridonian sandstone, now in a state of terminal decay. Only 612 m (2010 ft) high, this little hill has an aura out of all proportion to its size and occupies a place of special affection in the hearts of many Scottish climbers. Over-visited in summer because of its easy access (there is a large car park right at its foot) and because its summit, or at least the low point on the ridge, presents an easy objective, the mountain is a much lonelier place in winter when you are virtually certain of being alone. Near the warming influence of the sea and in the wet and variable West Highland winter, snow may come and go and never lasts very long even on the top of Stac Polly, but on the rare occasions when the ridge is sheathed in ice and snow, its traverse becomes a real adventure.

In summer, the cliffs of both the eastern and western summits provide good rock-climbing on warm red sandstone, and from almost any point on the ridge the view spans 360 degrees. South across Loch Lurgainn are the peaks of the Ben More Coigach range; northwards, Cul Mor, Canisp, Suilven, Quinag and a score of other peaks fade to the horizon; to the east, Stac Polly's nearest neighbour, Cul Beg, has a bold outline which, under a good covering of snow and with a little imagination, you can persuade yourself is very like Mount Everest; west, the moors slope gently to the Atlantic, about 8 km away.

CANISP AND SUILVEN

These two sandstone monoliths lift from the rolling uplands of west Sutherland, ringed by almost uncountable lochs and lochans. Of the two, Suilven is the lower but much the more dramatic, dominating its surroundings. It must be one of the most striking and best-known peaks in Britain and was named Pillar Mountain by the Norse for its end-on view from the west. The main summit, seen in the photograph, is named Caisteal Liath – 'the Grey Castle'. More recently, for the enormous rounded hump which it presents to Lochinver, the nearest village, it has been called the Sugar Loaf. When seen from the north or south, the view this gives of the length of the ridge with its triple peaks has been compared to a ship at anchor. Like many of the isolated mountains in this north-west corner of the Highlands, from a distance Suilven rears out of the moors like nothing so much as some prehistoric beast rising from the deep.

In this landscape without roads, all walks have to be carefully planned. Although the 8 km trek from the nearest public road to the foot of Suilven's ridge is straightforward, the locality is so interrupted by water that any attempt to make straight-line marches is doomed to failure. In a few square kilometres of the Inverpolly and Glencanisp estates around the base of the mountain, some two hundred lochs are crammed. The Cam Loch which winds around Suilven's southern and eastern slopes is more than 12 km long but only a few hundred metres wide; nearby Loch Sionascaig, which is less than 5 km long, has a shoreline of such complexity that it measures more than 26 km.

CHURCH HALL, ELPHIN

This little church hall by the roadside at Elphin could be the prototype for similar corrugated-iron constructions all over the Highlands; it is certainly an archetype. In all the crofting communities and townships – too small and scattered to be called villages – and there are many of them, there can be few that do not possess a church or village hall like this one. Perhaps only one thing exceeds the number of halls, and that is the lexicon of uses to which they are put. The hall is very often the focal point of the community, especially in the winter months – church meetings, Sunday school, Bible class, Women's Institute, badminton club, polling station, temporary classroom, rehearsal room, theatre, concert hall. The list is endless.

My parents moved from the Borders of Scotland to the Highlands when I was six years old, and my first really clear recollection of our new home is of being taken to a concert, put on by the local people, in our own little village hall. To a small child in a very strange place, the hall seemed a huge arena, crammed to bursting with hundreds, if not thousands, of people – many more than I had ever seen in one place before. I remember little of the concert itself, but the impression of the vast crowd is still very strong. Recently I went back to have a look at our old home and the village hall. Of course, it was tiny and a close replica of the hall in the photograph, though not so spruce. I doubt whether it could ever have held even fifty people.

A place like Elphin, sitting near a river on a tract of good land by an important road junction, gives mute testimony to the depopulation of the Highlands. In England and Wales, or even the south of Scotland, people and services would have gravitated to such a place and a market town become established, its eventual size and success probably defined by the amount of traffic at its crossroads. At Elphin, as elsewhere in the north, the simple lack of people has prevented this from happening. A dozen or so scattered crofts and cottages, the church hall, the schoolroom (no longer a school), a summer tea-room, a craft shop – these are Elphin today. Few locals, I suspect, would argue if you called it a backwater, but few, either, would want it any other way.

THE LEDMORE RIVER NEAR ELPHIN

Cattle stand in the Ledmore River, 1 km before its junction with the Cam Loch, part of a vast and complex interconnecting network of lochs, rivers and streams which eventually drains into the Atlantic via the Inverkirkaig River. Elphin and Inchnadamph benefit from local intrusions of limestone among the sour and acid soils and rocks which form most of the northern Highlands. As a result, here and at other localities with similar good fortune, an oasis of green appears in an otherwise rather sterile region, botanically speaking. Not only is there good grazing for sheep and cattle, and a small amount of arable farming, but in the uncultivated areas, rare and beautiful wild flowers and plants occur. On the nearby limestone cliffs at Inchnadamph, purple saxifrage, rare grasses and sedges, holly fern and mountain avens thrive in an island of fertility surrounded by peat-bog and heathery upland.

Cattle had been the mainstay of traditional Highland life long before sheep, other than small native breeds, made their appearance in the glens, and hardy crossbred cattle, raised for beef and milk, still have an important part in local husbandry. One of the varieties used in breeding is the original Highland cow, long-haired and long-horned, and able to withstand the length and rigours of the northern winter. Mixed with southern breeds that have more milk or better meat, the Highland injects the necessary hardiness to produce a race of cattle ideally suited to the needs of a modern Highland farm.

On a day of strong westerly winds, with clouds sweeping rapidly overhead, a patch of blue sky to the east let the March sun through for a moment as I waited for the cows to strike the right pose, which they held for precisely a second.

Sheep at Ledmore Junction

In the distance, low cloud skimmed the top of Cul Mor some 7 km away, and at 850 m (2790 ft) one of the highest of the Assynt hills. At Ledmore, a road junction between Elphin and Inchnadamph where the only buildings are a telephone kiosk and a distant cottage, a flock of sheep stood expectantly as if waiting to be fed, which perhaps they were.

More than any other single factor during the past two hundred years, sheep have changed the Highlands – the landscape, the way of life and the very population of the hills and glens. After the 1745 rebellion had been put down, and as Britain's population and involvement in foreign wars increased, the demand for meat from Highland cattle became so great that businessmen from the south began to lease tracts of land in the Highlands for grazing. Driven south to be sold at the huge cattle fairs at Falkirk, the animals became a source of profit not only to the cattlemen, but to the Highland chiefs whose lands they grazed. This alone led to many evictions as people were cleared from the land to make more room for cattle. Sad though this was, it bore no comparison to what was to come.

By the middle of the century, Border sheep were already grazing the green acres of Perthshire and Argyll, and in the 1760s, Sir John Lockhart-Ross of Balnagown in Ross and Cromarty introduced the first to be seen north of the Highland line. Others were quick to follow and, before the end of the century, flocks of Cheviot sheep were streaming up the same drove roads into the Highlands that the Black Cattle took on their journey south to the markets. The Cheviot was a superbly bred sheep and admirably adapted for life in the northern glens. Sheep could be raised twice as profitably as cattle on the same ground, even if the value of their wool was discounted; and the wool was more valuable than the meat. When the first few large-scale experiments were seen to be successful, the fate of the Highland people was sealed. They had no title to the land they occupied and tilled. Enabled to remain only by the grace of their chiefs and in return for military service, when that grace was withdrawn they had nowhere to turn. Throughout the Highlands a dreadful exodus began. Evicted and betrayed by their former protectors, the clan chiefs, their houses and crops burned behind them, bullied and beaten, they went meekly into exile. The age of the caoraich mhor – the Great Sheep – had arrived.

QUINAG, ACROSS LOCH A' CHAIRN BHAIN

Quinag (pronounced 'Koonyag') is the last and most northerly in the chain of mountains, constructed in Torridonian sandstone, which runs up the west coast of Scotland from Applecross in Inverness-shire. Widely visible from the roads running through the district of Assynt in which it stands, Quinag's isolation gives it an unquestioned grandeur, and like many other hills in the region it can be considered more a mountain range in miniature than a single peak. Quinag is 6 km long from north to south, and forms a great Y with the two northern arms – Sail Gharbh and Sail Ghorm – enclosing a huge bowl-shaped coire well over 300 m deep. The mountain has six separate summits over 700 m (2300 ft) and to the west shows an almost unbroken line of cliffs over 4 km long. The single most distinctive rock feature is Barrel Buttress, an impressive two-tiered set of cliffs over 365 m (1200 ft) high, split by deep vertical gullies and rising directly to the northern summit of Sail Ghorm. Climbing on this was pioneered in 1907, and the mountain has remained popular with walkers and climbers ever since, though rock-climbing now tends to be concentrated on the western cliffs.

On a clear day the views from the summit span the entire northern Highlands, with the mountains of Assynt and Coigach – Canisp, Suilven, Cul Mor, Cul Beag, Stac Polly and Ben More Coigach – crowding together dramatically to the south, and the Atlantic coast, deeply riven by sea lochs, fading away towards Cape Wrath to the north and the island of Skye to the south-west. In very clear conditions the Outer Hebrides can be seen along the horizon, as well as the snow caps of the Torridon and Kintail ranges.

LOCH STACK AND THE LAIRG TO LAXFORD ROAD

Driving from Laxford Bridge along the A838 – a narrow and twisting single track which the Scottish Department of Transport has the nerve to classify as an A road – Loch Stack is the first of several lochs that line the route. This road is one of only two that cross the vast territory of central Sutherland from east to west, plus one that cuts away to reach the north coast of the county at Tongue. All three radiate out from Lairg, a small agricultural centre at the head of the Rogart valley some 25 km from the east coast, and all are spectacular, the more so if heading in a westerly direction as the moorland of east-central Sutherland gives way to the mountains of Assynt. Loch Stack, like all the neighbouring lochs and rivers, is very popular with fishermen, and both salmon and trout abound in good years in these waters. The Duke of Westminster has large sporting estates in this part of Sutherland and his famous race-horses, Foinaven and Arkle, were named after mountains nearby.

The photograph was taken on New Year's Day some years ago, and a skim of snow covered the tops of Meallan Liath Coire Mhic Dhugaill about 10 km away, in centre frame. Even on a summer's day, the narrow roads across the interior never became busy as most visitors stick to the scenic coastal route, and in mid-winter you can drive for an hour and not see another vehicle. On the quietest day of the year in Scotland, I left Golspie on the east coast before daybreak with plans to do some climbing, and I saw no one all the way to Loch Stack, a drive of some 80 km. Unfortunately this turned out to be my only picture of the day since, within minutes of taking the shot, rain was teeming down and other plans had to be abandoned.

HEILIM, LOCH ERIBOLL

Driving along the north coast from Durness towards Caithness, the road twice swings inland to bypass the ends of fjords which bite deeply into the land. The first of these is Loch Eriboll, a lonely and windswept loch, and on the 25 km detour around its shores no village, and barely a house, is to be seen. Unlike the fjords of the west coast, those in the north are not surrounded by high mountains. For most of its length Loch Eriboll is flanked by rolling moorland and low hills reaching a maximum height of around 400 m (1310 ft). Near its southern end, however, crags rise above the shore and the mountains are not far away. To the west the moors rise gently to the green and rounded summits of Cranstackie and Beinn Spionnadh, whose easy slopes make fine walking terrain. To the south lies the high and lonely mountain country of Foinaven and Arkle, whose summits of white Cambrian quarzite can gleam like snow.

Loch Eriboll became known to many British sailors during the last war when its deep and safe waters were used as an anchorage and assembly point for Altantic convoys. The loch was said to be deep and large enough to shelter the entire British Navy. Few, if any, reminders of this period in its history are visible today. Eriboll has one of the very few breeding colonies, on the Scottish mainland, of the grey seal. Though they breed around the coasts of Wales and Ireland, and in north Cornwall, in Scottish waters they tend to confine themselves to uninhabited islands or the more remote beaches of inhabited ones. The seaward end of Loch Eriboll, however, is relatively far from any human habitation. The cliffs have caves providing shelter for both pups and nursing mothers, and the small but significant colony produces up to a hundred calves each year.

BEACH AT SANGOBEG

The north-coast beaches of Sutherland and Caithness are stunning and probably only the climate has saved them from the kind of development that has ruined similar coasts all around the world. Nevertheless, on a still summer's evening the azure water can look as inviting as it would anywhere, though its temperature will quickly remind anyone who does venture in that they are very definitely in northern latitudes. Once you step off the beach there is nothing but sea between you and the Polar ice cap, and the oceanic breakers rolling in to the beach at Sangobeg confirm this. (The dot on the beach is a strolling couple and the waves are nearly 2 m high.) The cliffs and stacks of Whiten Head, standing out against the horizon, are nearly 150 m (490 ft) high at their highest, and are composed of tough gneiss and quartzite rocks.

The nearest village, Durness, is just a few kilometres along the coast. It is famous mainly for Smoo Cave, a huge cavern entered from the beach just below the hotel. Durness gave its name to the vein of limestone that occurs here and there up the north-west coast, for example at Elphin, and is equally favoured with a fertile environment which can support a decent-sized community. The local rock being limestone is also the reason for the existence of Smoo Cave, hollowed out of the water-soluble rock by the waters of the Allt Smoo, a stream which runs just 2 km to the sea from its source in Loch Meadaidh. The river goes underground just south of the road, to emerge as a waterfall in one of the two inner chambers of the cave. There are three chambers altogether, of which the outer and most accessible is the largest at 10 m high and 65 m long. Smoo has been visited by many celebrities, of whom the first recorded was perhaps Sir Walter Scott in 1814.

THE FLOW COUNTRY, NEAR KINBRACE

At the head of The Strath of Kildonan, briefly famous for its gold rush during the 1860s, the lonely little settlement of Kinbrace lies on the southern fringes of a vast tract of moor and low, rolling hills that have become popularly known as the Flow Country. The landscape was first formed in pre-glacial times as sedimentary rock, but its geology is immensely complex, with repeated folding of the strata, metamorphism, and frequent intrusions of rocks of other types and ages. It is a puzzle even geologists find difficult to comprehend. The present shape of the land was heavily influenced in the last major glaciation when a huge ice cap formed in central Sutherland, with the primary flow movements towards the north and east coasts. This created a great rolling tableland of rock, much of which the later melting of the ice cap and glaciers was to cover with a layer of debris called 'till'. Later, a layer of peat was laid down over most of the area. Long thought to be merely an uninteresting expanse of blanket bog, the Flow Country is now recognized as an important refuge for many plant and insect species threatened elsewhere as wetlands are progressively drained and reclaimed. Rare and specialized communities of grasses, sedges, mosses and heaths coexist with the more common species of heather, cotton grass and deer grass. Insectivorous plants such as sundew and butterwort thrive here, and on higher, better-drained ground there is bearberry, cloudberry, and dwarf cornel and birch. Though the area had been extensively grazed by sheep and deer, keeping tree growth to a mini-mum, it was known that islands in lochs, even when composed of this rather poor soil, were able to support trees. Plantations were begun as early as the nineteenth century, and it was soon found that some species of conifer did well enough if protected from grazing animals by a deer fence. In more recent times the Forestry Commission has been the major force in new planting throughout Sutherland, but controversy arose in the 1980s when new Government subsidies and tax breaks made investment in forestry very attractive to well-to-do private individuals. Media figures became involved in schemes to plant the Flow Country and for a time the affair acquired wide notoriety. However, the establishment of several Sites of Special Scientific Interest in the region, together with changes in the tax laws, has taken some of the pressure off the Flow Country.

THE RIMSDALE BURN, BADANLOCH

In a landscape absolutely typical of this part of Sutherland, the Rimsdale Burn, swollen by a rapid thaw after heavy snow, wanders south from its origins in the peaty wetlands a few kilometres from where it crosses the B871, the Kinbrace to Bettyhill road. The stream meanders down the centre of a narrow but absolutely flat miniature valley, to run into the complex of interconnected lochs – Rimsdale, nan Clar and Badanloch – from which the Helmsdale, an important salmon-fishing river, rises. In the distance, the gently contoured massif of Ben Armine is cloud-capped. Huge in area but rising to only 712 m (2340 ft), its lower slopes are heavily planted with young conifer forest. Ben Armine is remote from any public road and of little interest to climbers and walkers, except for the broad vistas from its summit over the great expanse of northern moorland. Deer are hunted over most of this area, and in the past Ben Armine, like other parts of central Sutherland, was known for its grouse shoots. Grouse have declined dramatically, however, as estates have given up the widespread artificial management of the heather moorland. On the nearby Ben Griam estate, thousands of grouse were shot annually during the late nineteenth century, as well as large numbers of mountain ('blue') hares. Indiscriminate heather-burning, over-grazing by sheep, forestry plantation and the management of the estates for deer rather than grouse have combined drastically to reduce the quantity and quality of heather on which both the birds and the hares are so dependent.

In the middle distance the short, hummocky hills ('drumlins') are characteristic of river valleys throughout the region. These are mounds of glacial debris, deposited at the end of the last ice age and redistributed by fast-flowing glacial streams that carved the valleys through which today's rivers run.

Thurso, near Cooper Square

In modern times, Thurso, like many other places, has had to come to terms with some drastically changed circumstances. As its traditional trade with Scandinavia fell in volume and the great ports of southern Britain rose to pre-eminence through the nineteenth century, other industries had to be found to keep the town alive. In Caithness there are enormous deposits of flagstone lying in horizontal beds which had been quarried since prehistoric times. Commercial quarrying began around the late 1790s, and by 1825 Mr James Traill was exporting dressed flagstones from his cutting and polishing yards on the banks of the Thurso River. The trade continued well into the twentieth century, and flagstones were sent as far afield as Canada and Australia. In Thurso, extensive building use was made of flagstones, including the harbour. Undressed stone was used as fences, and even twenty-five years ago most fields and roads were lined with Caithness flags. Today, sadly, the trade has diminished and though a few quarries are worked on a small scale, the miles of flagstone fencing have virtually disappeared as modern replacements became cheaper and easier to maintain.

Latterly, Thurso has become something of a tourist resort, but, with its position on the coast and with the nearby deep-water harbour at Scrabster, Thurso will always have strong maritime connections and there is still a strong fishing tradition. Though many boats now base themselves at Scrabster, there is a home fleet of seine-netters and foreign boats also make use of the facilities. The ferry trade to and from Orkney brings a lot of business to Thurso, and the coming of Dounreay, only a few kilometres along the coast, has given continuing employment to many local people.

THE HARBOUR, WICK

This is another town whose origins go back at least to Viking days, and the town was mentioned in the Orkneyinga Sagas as early as 1140 when Earl Rognvald was entertained there. The name is from the Old Norse 'vik', meaning bay, and the town probably came into being because of the wide river mouth which gives the only sheltered anchorage from all but northeast winds down a long stretch of this east coast. It was created a royal burgh in 1589, though it was then no more than a straggle of houses and a church on the north shores of the river. By the mid-eighteenth century it had become an important fishing station, with more than two hundred herring boats based there and extensive curing and smoking sheds along the riverbank. In 1803 the British Fisheries Society decided to improve the port, and Thomas Telford was commissioned to build a new town and harbour on the south side of the river. There were fine new streets of houses on the higher ground, and a complex of smoking and curing sheds. The area was called Pulteneytown after its champion, Sir William, and retains the name today. Further alterations and additions were made in the 1860s under Thomas Stevenson, and Wick continued to prosper throughout the nineteenth century despite the beginning of a decline in the herring fisheries. The area around Wick has many historical associations, and there are numerous ruined castles and fortified houses in the vicinity. Along the coast between Wick and John o' Groats, excavations have shown that some of the earliest settlements in Scotland were here and, though nothing remains visible today, archaeological traces of Middle Stone Age culture have been found. The coastline is also very scenic both north and south of Wick, with high cliffs and dramatic sea stacks teeming with bird life.

The Caithness Coast at Berriedale

A fine shingle beach lies below a rocky headland where the confluence of the Langwell and Berriedale Waters meets the sea. On the last stage of their journeys from the lower slopes of Morven and Scaraben – Caithness's highest hills, just inland from Berriedale – both streams run through thickly wooded valleys before meeting close to the shore-line. This whole length of coast is extremely rocky and is interrupted by numerous deep ravines. The main road, as a result, is both narrow and winding, and Berriedale Hill used to be a byword for extremely difficult driving conditions, especially in winter. A road improvement scheme at Berriedale and better brakes on modern cars have taken some of the terrors out of this particular stretch, where the road used to descend very steeply into the river gorge before climbing just as steeply out again. In icy conditions it really was a fearsome test of a driver's nerve and accidents used to be common. There are still other sections near Berriedale that require some care, but nothing quite as demanding.

The village's other claim to fame used to be the post office, whose exterior walls were extravagantly decorated with stags' antlers. Near the sea there are scanty ruins of a fourteenth-century castle, a stronghold of the earls of Caithness, but the immediate area is of most interest for its wild coastline and the abundance of sea birds which congregate on the many cliffs. Some kilometres down the coast towards Helmsdale, the Ord of Caithness (the southern limit of the county) was a place of ill omen to the ruling Sinclair family. They never crossed it on a Monday, after a large number of the clan's menfolk went south on that day to fight at Flodden, from where none came back alive.

ROCK SKERRIES NEAR PORTGOWER

At midday in mid-winter in these northern latitudes the sun barely seems to clear the horizon; by mid-afternoon, when this photograph was taken, it was already far on its downward journey, and in another hour it would be twilight. By 4.00 p.m.–4.30 p.m. at the latest – it would be dark. These terribly brief hours of winter daylight are compensated by long light at midsummer: in June there are at least eighteen hours of good daylight and in really fine weather it never gets properly dark. The other factor that makes up for short days in winter is the quality of the light, which on a clear day of sun and blue sky is really beautiful from before sun-up until well after sunset.

On a February day spent walking the quiet, empty beaches of east Sutherland, the soft light of an afternoon sun glistening from the waters of the Moray Firth epitomized this perfectly. For more than 20 km, from Golspie in the south to Portgower in the north, the coast is a series of strands of white or golden sand interspersed by brief rocky stretches and miniature headlands. On any day in winter you could walk the more remote of these beaches and never see a living soul. On my solitary walk a few cormorants lifted away from the rocks as I approached; grey seals bobbed in the swell a few metres offshore and waited, no doubt, until I was long gone before hauling back up on the sand to doze in the weak sunshine; the long rock skerries took on the shapes of U-boats as they submerged beneath the oncoming tide. On the horizon, a thin dark line of land along the far shores of the Firth faded behind the rising haze of an early dusk.

ABANDONED BARN, GLEN LOTH

On the A9 between Brora and Helmsdale, near to where a stone has been erected to the last wolf killed in Sutherland, a lonely little road, unmarked on most maps, cuts away north west into the hills. This is Glen Loth, and the road leads through a lonely and atmospheric glen below Beinn Dhorain, the highest hill in east Sutherland, to cross a pass over 300 m (980 ft) high. From the summit of the pass, on a fine day, there is a view far to the north of Morven and Scaraben, the hills of east Caithness. The hills here are of Old Red Sandstone with rounded contours that are easy on the eye, and the soil is of a type which does not form peat, but provides good pasture. Sheltered from the cold east wind, the little valley is a suntrap, with temperatures often several degrees above the surrounding area. On a warm summer's day, with only the buzz of insects to disturb the silence, there seems much that is idyllic here. Several types of pre-historic dwelling have been found in the glen: there are the remains of a broch or Pictish tower, and the ruins of several crofts lie in the rank grass of untended fields. Today, no one lives in Glen Loth. It was cleared of people in 1809 and 1813 by Patrick Sellar, factor for Lord Stafford, Duke of Sutherland, and has never again been inhabited.

Wolves survived in Sutherland into historical times and there are well-documented records of them in the county in the early seventeenth century. The Glen Loth wolves were eradicated by a hunter named Polson and, though it is not known for sure where and when the last one died, it seems that the last few were in Assynt in the west of the county, in Strath Halladale in the north and here in Glen Loth. They were eliminated between 1690 and 1700, just a century before the human populations of these glens were to suffer a similar fate.

THE MORAY FIRTH AT LOTH

The crofting and farming township of Loth straggles for several kilometres along the east coast of Sutherland, between Brora and Helmsdale, without ever coming together as a recognizable village. Though there used to be a primary school, village hall and a post office, I don't think any of these still exist. My family moved there when I was six and, though we stayed for only a year before moving to Golspie just down the coast, I still have very fond memories of Loth and always visit it when in the area. The beaches are wonderful, but most require some knowledge of how to reach them plus a fair bit of walking as they are not near the main road. This, and the total lack of any local hotel accommodation (and not much b&b) has kept them totally unspoilt. Near Crackaig Farm at the south end of Loth, camping and caravanning are permitted on one piece of foreshore, but facilities are minimal and the site is always quiet. Even on a warm summer's day, if you know where to go, you can have a couple of kilometres of beach all to yourself; except, that is, for a prolific wildlife which can include grey seals, shelduck, eider duck, great northern divers, arctic and sandwich terns, and a whole range of gulls and waders. The photograph was taken on a winter's day when there was less bird life around, but on many stretches of beach numerous seals were hauled out and dozing on the sands. Cormorants perched on rocky islets and skerries drying their outstretched wings but, like the seals, fled at the first sign of a human presence.

During the last war there was some fear that an invasion could come through these remote north-eastern beaches, and elaborate defences and early-warning systems were organized. In some places, lines of huge concrete barriers – 'tank-traps' – were set up, and in others there were chains of look-out posts and radar positions. At Loth the latter is the case, and the rudimentary concrete buildings still dot the foreshore and headlands for several kilometres where the open waters and gently sloping beaches would have allowed easy landings from the sea. Inland there were command positions and gun emplacements, some now used for storage by local farmers but most disused and just mouldering away. Further south, where the narrow coastal strip was just wide enough, there were several airfields; but the invasion never came.

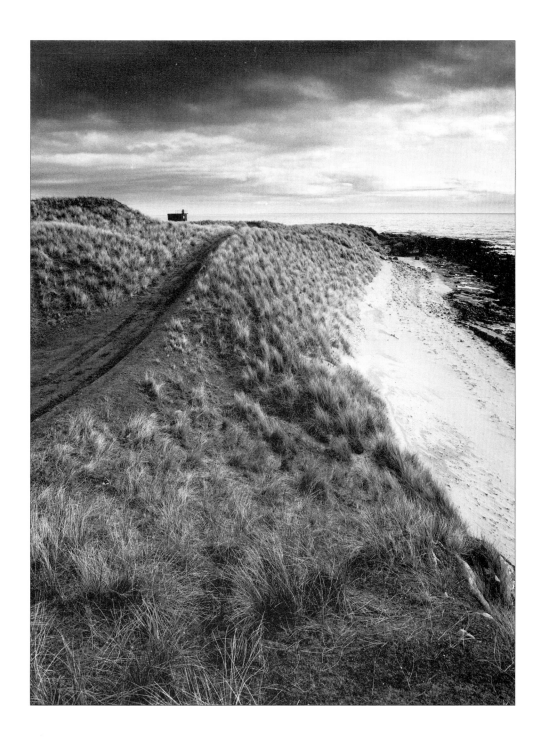

DUNROBIN CASTLE, GOLSPIE

About 2 km north of Golspie and just off the main A9 coast road, at the end of an impressive drive flanked by tall beech trees, Dunrobin Castle is the seat of the ducal Sutherland family. The earliest record of some form of tower or fortification on the site dates from around 1275, when a square turreted tower was built by Robert, 2nd Earl of Sutherland. The area was in a state of turmoil for long periods, with three families – the Sutherlands, the Mackays and the Gordons – vying for control of the whole Moray Firth region, as the high number of castles, keeps and fortified houses around this coast testifies. It was many centuries after the first building at Dunrobin before ruling Highland families felt able to live in unfortified mansions and to indulge a taste for architecture rather than defence. Though over the years the basic structure of Dunrobin was much added to, its original purpose as a fortress was kept intact, and the appearance of the present castle, in an elaborate French 'chateau' style with large formal gardens, dates from only the nineteenth century. It does incorporate earlier construction, and elements from the sixteenth, seventeenth and eighteenth centuries are still present. The castle is open to the public and contains a magnificent collection of furniture and tapestries, and paintings by Canaletto, Reynolds and Ramsay. It saw a spell as a naval hospital during the First World War when, unfortunately, it was extensively damaged by fire, and more recently as a boys school – a commercial venture which did not survive long.

The castle grounds contain many fascinating lesser buildings: old workers' cottages, an icehouse, a large dovecote, a museum and formerly a private harbour which was sadly destroyed in an easterly gale some years ago. The museum, which was built in 1723, contains relics relating to the castle and its history, as well as objects and arte-facts of local interest. The most important collection is of carved Pictish symbol stones, all of which were found in east Sutherland.

'PALM BEACH', GOLSPIE, EAST SUTHERLAND

Along the eastern seaboard of Ross-shire and Sutherland, a narrow coastal strip, fertile and intensively farmed, separates the Moray Firth from the moors and mountains of the interior. At Golspie it is particularly narrow, with just space for the village to squeeze between the shore and the lower slopes of Ben Bhraggie. The hill is crowned by a 30 m monument (to a former Duke of Sutherland) which is either a beloved landmark or an eyesore, depending on your viewpoint, and a story circulates that renegade Scottish Nationalists once tried to dynamite it, though without visible effect. South of Golspie the coastal plain widens and a sandy beach runs for 5 km to the mouth of the River Fleet. Halfway along this beach, just above the sands, a group of Scots pines stands, in splendid decay, among the bent-grass. This the locals have dubbed Palm Beach. Behind the trees a large area of virgin land, barely rising above sea-level, is home to rare mosses and lichens which depend for their existence on periodic flooding with saltwater during storms and spring tides. Once a favourite picnic spot, the area has been designated a Site of Special Scientific Interest, reachable only by a long trek on foot since cars are now banned. The old trees, climbed by generations of Golspie children, are now strictly a no-go zone.

Nearby, the estuary of the River Fleet, which drains at low tide, provides a habitat of international importance for waders and wildfowl, both native and migratory. Herons patrol its shallows, and seals and occasionally porpoises can be seen in the tide-rip where the estuary empties through narrows into the sea.

Sunset over Loch Fleet

At low tide the afterglow of sunset reflected across the sands and mudflats of one of the most important bird habitats in the Moray Firth region. Loch Fleet is a shallow tidal estuary which has been almost completely closed off by the growth of sand and shingle bars across its mouth. Only the rapid tidal movement, as the estuary fills and empties, keeps the narrow exit channel open. The shallow waters, and the huge area of mudflat which is exposed at low tide, make Loch Fleet a feeding station of the greatest importance to both migratory and native birds. Various species of duck form the major communities, with winter being the peak season for numbers. Though some species are, of course, native to the UK, and others breed here, it is the vast flocks of over-wintering birds that bring bird-watchers to Loch Fleet from all over Britain. Mallard, teal, widgeon, pintail, shoveller, tufted duck, scaup, goldeneye and pochard all winter here, and the more common species can sometimes be seen in flocks numbering hundreds. In October and November, sea duck begin to arrive, and eiders, scoters and long-tails form great rafts of thousands of birds, sometimes in the estuary itself, but more commonly in the open sea, just offshore from the mouth. The mudflats are, of course, attractive to all types of wading birds, and the common species are oystercatcher, dunlin, godwit, curlew, redshank, knot, sanderling and golden plover. Many other species can be seen from time to time, and even rare North American species make an occasional appearance. Many of these waders also nest on the quieter beaches around the estuary.

Loch Fleet's present shape is partly due to human intervention. In 1813, Thomas Telford bridged the Kyle of Sutherland at Bonar Bridge, and in 1816 built a causeway (ever after called 'The Mound') to carry a road across the inner end of the estuary. The road still crosses the causeway today, and for many years a branchline of the railway, to Dornoch, also used it. At the time of building it was hoped to reclaim the land cut off from the sea by the causeway but, because of the large volumes of water coming down the River Fleet, this was impossible. Instead, the area has become colonized by willow and alder. Today it is the largest natural alderwood in Scotland, a Site of Special Scientific Interest, and a National Nature Reserve.

THE FREE CHURCH OF SCOTLAND, LAIRG

So typical of the Highlands, especially the northern Highlands, is the plain and simple outline of many a Free Church building. This one at Lairg with its belfry and attached manse is more decorative than some. Inside these churches, plain wooden pews and an unadorned interior without stained glass in the windows speaks of a form of worship from which all inessentials and embellishments have been removed. The Free Church movement in Scotland has its origins in the 1730s and '40s when a new and popular brand of evangelical preaching began to be heard. This was often delivered by lay preachers and led in many places to congregations deserting the Established Church in favour of these fiery laymen. As the eighteenth century progressed, ministers of the Established Church were increasingly identified, in the minds of their parishioners, with the ideas and even the practices of their feudal lords – the clan chiefs and their agents – who were already beginning what was to become infamous as The Highland Clearances. As the ministers became more and more the apologists of the landowners, so the evangelicals became more anti-landlord. The decisive break came in 1843 with the Disruption. The 'Free Protesting Church of Scotland' was formed, and in Sutherland alone it is thought that nearly seventy per cent of the total population joined the new church. Immediately the problems between landowners and tenants were exacerbated. They now did not even worship in the same church, and each side heard its own prejudices echoing back to it, on Sundays, from the pulpit. It is hard to say whether the formation of their own church actually helped the crofters' situation, but at least they did not have to listen to sermons extolling the virtues of their tormentors or urging them to emigrate.

Later, even the Free Church faced schisms, and the Free Presbyterian Church and the United Free Church emerged from within its ranks. But for a long time they all helped keep going the old landlord–tenant suspicion and rivalry, and even today the churchgoers of many villages separate on Sundays into two communities, with the descendants of the old professional classes and tenant farmers, newcomers from the south and present-day professionals going to the Church of Scotland, while the old crofting and fishing families go to the Free Church.

Oil Rigs in the Cromarty Firth

The discovery of oil in Scottish waters during the early 1970s brought new industries and a new prosperity to some parts of the Highlands. Around the coastline, at various points, rig-building yards sprang up: at Cromarty on the tip of the Black Isle, at Kishorn in West Inverness-shire and at Nigg near Aberdeen. Many other east-coast locations saw the benefits of the rig-servicing industry as oil exploration got into full swing, and here in the Cromarty Firth just north of Inverness, the little town of Invergordon was the local nucleus.

Alongside the traditional industries of the area – farming, fishing, whisky production and tourism – oil companies, engineering yards and rig servicing outfits set up shop, and the region saw a rapid influx of new population and expertise. The local economy boomed and unemployment fell dramatically in the favoured localities, but, as the 1980s progressed, higher oil taxes and a falling oil price combined to make exploration, always a high-risk business, less and less attractive to the major oil companies. For some years now the Cromarty Firth has simply provided a safe and sheltered anchorage for a fleet of moth-balled exploration rigs, laid up against a time when conditions may become more favourable. The yards are closed, the hordes of oil-industry experts have departed and unemployment is again high. The rigs now do little more than provide a dramatic and unexpected scene in the midst of some otherwise tranquil east-coast lowland landscapes. The helicopter hovering over the nearer rig provides only the illusion of activity – it was mine, chartered to look the part for a picture in an advertising campaign.

URQUHART CASTLE AND LOCH NESS

The castle sits in a stunning position at the end of a craggy promontory on the northern shores of the loch. Once the largest castle in Scotland, it is now substantially ruined and perhaps the more romantic for it. This is another site that has been fortified since prehistory and archaeological examinations have found traces of an Iron Age fort here. The present ruins date to the early sixteenth century, when Clan Grant came into possession of the castle and built most of what remains. It was blown up in 1692 to prevent it from becoming a Jacobite stronghold.

Loch Ness is, of course, famous worldwide for the monster more than for its beauty. It is nearly 40 km long and a little over 1 km wide, on average, and this extraordinary length and narrowness, combined with the low containing hills, do not make for memorable scenery when compared to other Highland lochs. But what it may lack in this department is more than compensated for by the legend of the loch and its monster, whose first recorded sighting was in the seventh century by no less an authority than St Columba. Whatever the truth or otherwise of its existence (and scientific expeditions and surveys have failed to prove the matter either way), a considerable industry has been built on the creature's back and no one in the tourist trade along Loch Ness-side is going to admit to even a moment's doubt in the matter. But the most hardened sceptic still finds it hard to avert the eyes from those dark and often mysterious waters, whose 270 m depths may easily hide discoveries still to be made and species unknown to science.

Not far from the castle, a cairn commemorates the death of the racing driver, John Cobb, who was killed on Loch Ness during an attempt on the world waterspeed record in September 1952.

KESSOCK BRIDGE, INVERNESS

The Kessock narrows, which divide the Moray Firth from the inner, land-locked waters of the Beauly Firth, also separate Inverness, the 'capital' of the Highlands, from the fertile peninsula of the Black Isle and the shortest road-route to the far north. Since the Middle Ages, at least, the narrows have been crossed by a ferry and for most of this century this has been a car ferry. But as with many places on the west coast of the Highlands, bridge-building spelt the end for the ferry service. When the Kessock Bridge opened in 1980 another link with the past was gone. North Kessock, the village on the north shore where the ferry landed, was formerly a crofting and fishing village of some charm, but with the speed and ease of crossing via the new bridge it is now a burgeoning dormitory for Inverness. The town is very much the administrative and industrial capital of the Highlands, with good road, rail, sea and air communications. The headquarters of the Highland Regional Council are here, together with the offices of Highlands & Islands Enterprise, and the National Trust for Scotland and Scottish Nature. It lies at the eastern terminus of the Caledonian Canal, and only a mile or two from the end of Loch Ness, whose fame alone draws tourists by the thousand. Mountains and beautiful scenery are relatively distant, but Inverness has different attractions on offer and the town has a considerable history.

Castle Hill in the centre of the burgh above the River Ness, has carried fortifications since the sixth century AD: the town appears in the Viking sagas and the castle was the site of Duncan's murder in Shakespeare's *Macbeth*. Inverness was fought over, or occupied by, English armies of occupation during the Scottish War of Independence, by Robert the Bruce, Mary Queen of Scots, Cromwell, the forces of the Restoration, and by the Jacobites in 1715 and '45. The then castle was destroyed to prevent further use as a garrison and the present Victorian edifice was built in the years after 1834. There are many other buildings and relics with historic connections going back as far as 500 BC, and the town's medieval origins are readily seen in its network of narrow streets which can create traffic problems. Not long ago the main north–south and east–west roads went through the centre of Inverness; from the resulting chaos the Kessock Bridge grew.

RUTHVEN BARRACKS

A mile outside Kingussie, and visible from far and wide up and down this part of the Spey valley, Ruthven Barracks stand on a large knoll which was originally the site of a medieval castle. This had been the stronghold of the notoriously cruel and warlike 'Wolf of Badenoch', the second son of King Robert II of Scotland, who held the region for the crown. The barracks were built in the aftermath of the first Jacobite Rebellion of 1715, one of four major military strongholds positioned around the Highlands and intended to subdue the clans. One hundred and twenty infantrymen were garrisoned here at first, and the buildings were later enlarged and a stable block added to permit the housing of mounted troops. When General Wade undertook his programme of military road-building in the Highlands, Ruthven found itself at the junction of three of these roads and its strategic importance was greatly enhanced. As a result, in the second rebellion of 1745, the castle was immediately a target for the Jacobite forces and was attacked by them on their march south, though successfully defended against great odds. On their return march north the Jacobites had brought captured artillery, and the stronghold fell to them and was destroyed. Later, after the catastrophic defeat at Culloden, the pathetic survivors of Prince Charles Edward Stuart's army gathered at Ruthven in the hope that their campaign could somehow be continued. Instead they received from the Prince only the brief instruction: 'Let every man seek his own safety in the best way he can.'

Today, the gaunt and unlovely ruin stands as an apt reminder of that bleak period in the history of the Highlands.

THE AVIEMORE CENTRE

It is tempting, but unkind, to label some of the buildings of the Aviemore Centre as a kind of modern barracks. As an artefact of the 1960s its architecture, by modern standards, leaves a lot to be desired, though there is no doubt that it took winter sports in Scotland from being a minority pursuit, enjoyed by a tiny elite, to one of mass participation. It has the distinction of being Europe's first purpose-built leisure and sports centre; more famous and glamourous resorts such as Les Arcs in the French Alps came much later. The Centre has undergone several additions and facelifts since its inception, and its facilities today include hotels, restaurants, shops, cinema, theatre, ice rink, swimmimg pool, go-kart track and dry ski-slope. With the more traditional range of facilities on offer in the village of Aviemore itself, the Craigellachie Nature Reserve immediately behind the Centre, sophisticated hotel accommodation at nearby Coylumbridge, the mountain skills training centre at Glenmore Lodge, water sports on Loch Morlich and the Cairngorm ski-slopes themselves, Aviemore has a comprehensive range of year-round activities for the visitor. In spite of that – and this is a purely personal comment – it is a hard place to like. The Centre is curiously soulless, and the original village has undergone such drastic changes and expansion that it is quite unrecognizable as the quiet Highland spa it used to be. However, a sweeping modernization programme has been planned and the Centre may yet rise anew, like the phoenix, from the ashes of its outdated 1960s tower blocks.

ROTHIEMURCHUS FOREST NEAR LOCH AN EILAN

In the wide basin of the Spey valley which lies between the Cairngorms and the lower hills north-west of Aviemore, there still remain considerable tracts of the old Scots pine forests of Glenmore and Rothiemurchus, which themselves were once part of the ancient forest of Caledon, and along with these wild woods of pine, birch and juniper, there are now large new plantations of spruce and fir. Several sizable lochs are scattered along the valley floor, of which Loch Morlich is the largest and Loch an Eilan the most romantic. Through the centre of all this runs the River Spey, and the Cairngorms provide a constant background to a landscape of great natural beauty whose combination of forest, water and mountain in ideal proportions has made the area one of Scotland's most popular holiday destinations. Red squirrel and roe deer are the typical animals of the pine and birch forests which support a wealth of birdlife including blackcock and capercaillie. Some years ago, reindeer were introduced into the northern Cairngorms on an experimental basis and a herd has now become established. In the Abernethy Forest just a few miles further up the valley, Loch Garten became famous in the 1960s and '70s as the site of the first nesting ospreys in Britain since they were exterminated in the early years of the century. The story of the near-extinction of this beautiful and harmless bird, which feeds exclusively on fish, is a tragic one. Beginning in the early nineteenth century, in less than a hundred years it was ruthlessly hunted out by a combination of estate gamekeepers and egg-collectors. When a pair of birds reappeared in the 1950s and after several years nested successfully, the eggs they produced were stolen by collectors. The species is making a slow and steady comeback but, even today, known nesting sites are still either kept secret or watched around the clock to protect them from these senseless and selfish people.

Loch an Eilan itself is an exceptionally pretty loch fringed by the pine-woods of Rothiemurchus forest and with a backdrop of dark hills. A pleasant path runs for 4 km around the loch, on whose single small island a ruined fifteenth-century castle stands.

INSH CHURCH, KINCRAIG

Just south of the village on a minor road, this little church, another archetype of the Highlands, stands in a grove of stately pine trees on a hillock. Below the trees and beyond a bend the River Spey begins to broaden into Loch Insh. The situation has every appearance of being auspicious and there are claims that this has been a sacred site since pre-Christian times. Druids are supposed to have used it for worship, and seen from the top of the knoll, the combination of water, trees and sky makes it a natural cathedral fit for any religion. In the dawn of the Christian era in Scotland, the first church here was said to have been established with the coming of the earliest missionaries in the sixth or seventh centuries. Today inside the church a very ancient Celtic bell gives some credence to these claims, and a hollowed-out stone font is supposed to have been used by St Adamnan, a contemporary of St Columba who founded his famous mission on the island of Iona, in the inner Hebrides.

The Highland Wildlife Park is nearby at Kincraig, where animals of Scotland's past as well as present – bison, deer, wildcats, wolves, bears and eagles (around sixty species in total) are displayed.

The region is one of the most scenic in Scotland, with the River Spey winding its way down the centre of a wide valley dotted with lochs and densely forested with both old woodlands and newer plantations. The whole is seen against the backdrop of the rolling Cairngorm mountains, frequently snow-capped even in summer, lying, on a fine day, beneath immense skies. It is also the prime outdoor sporting area in the Highlands, with salmon-fishing on the Spey, sailing and canoeing on the lochs, and walking, climbing and skiing in the Cairngorms.

THE NORTHERN CAIRNGORMS

Unlike any other group of Scottish mountains, the Cairngorms, with their great rolling domes and vast plateaus, form by far the greatest area of high upland in Britain, and the only incidence of true Arctic/Alpine conditions apart from the summit plateau of Ben Nevis. Spreading 40 km east–west and 25 km north–south, they comprise the largest group of high summits in Scotland, with four – Cairn Toul, Braeriach, Ben Macdui and Cairn Gorm – exceeding 1220 m (4000 ft) in height, several others coming close to that figure and a huge area of the Cairngorm plateau being higher than 1000 m (3280 ft). Everything here is on a vast scale and distances are great. This has led to tragedies when hill-walking parties have underestimated the potential ferocity of a Cairngorm blizzard and have pushed on in the face of deteriorating weather. In winter, storms can sweep in with terrifying speed and may last for days; the high plateau is without shelter of any kind and can be swept entirely clear of snow by the wind, so that even emergency snow-holes or igloos cannot be built. For mountaineers there is the frequent danger of avalanche, since much of the snow that falls on the summits gets swept by the wind into the corries where it builds up to great depths.

The photograph was taken from just below the summit of Cairn Gorm looking south-west to the distant summits of Cairn Toul, Angel Peak and Braeriach, which lie beyond the great trench of the Lairig Ghru (invisible in this view), the great pass which cuts through the Cairngorms from east to west. In the foreground, stony slopes thickly crusted with ice crystals lead down towards Coire an t-Sneachda and beyond the long dark ridge, to Coire an Lochan, two favourite climbing grounds on this northern rim of the Cairngorms.

PHOTOGRAPHIC NOTES

I tend to believe in simplicity of method in most things, and certainly in photography. Though the demands of a career in commercial photography mean that I have to work with all formats and styles of camera, from 35 mm to 10 in. x 8 in., in my personal work I prefer to reduce things to a reasonable minimum. To paraphrase a Japanese saying about food, if I could work happily with only 'one camera, one lens, one film' then I would. In practice this isn't really possible, but I do at least concentrate on one camera system at a time, and you get the best out of film by using one type consistently and getting to know what it can and can't do. In my early days in photography, I was a much more active climber than I am now and tended to use 35 mm for shots 'on the hill', for obvious reasons. I still do, on a rare outing on a rock or ice-climb, but don't use 35 mm for much else these days. When hill-walking, or any kind of walking, I find I can cope with the greater weight of a medium-format camera system (and tripod). For a long time I used the Hasselblad system; but for some years now I have used Pentax 67 and find the rectangular format more sympathetic to most landscapes. I also use a 5 in. x 4 in. system a great deal and it is my favourite but, unless you are Superman, it's not really a walker's camera; even if you can keep the weight down, the bulk of the camera itself, plus film-holders, lenses and accessories, doesn't sit well in a rucksack. So I use it near the car or when only a modicum of walking is involved. As a result, on a trip I generally take only the medium-format system or the 5 in. x 4 in., occasionally both, but never more than that. I keep filters to a minimum. For black-and-white I may use a yellow-green filter to lighten foliage and slightly darken a blue sky; in autumn and winter an orange filter will lighten the russets and browns of the landscape and improve the contrast between hill and sky. Otherwise I simply keep an 81A filter on all my lenses for protection against knocks and as a UV screen. In recent years I have standardized on Agfapan 100 film and generally print on Agfa Record Rapid paper, untoned.

Birch Saplings, Loch Hope

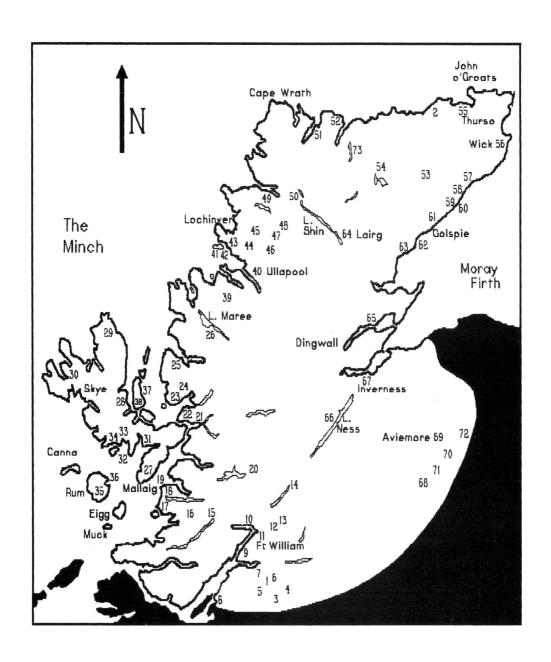

TECHNICAL DATA

PAGE NO.	MAP NO.	TITLE	CAMERA	LENS	FILM	STOP	SPEED	FILTER
iii	1	COW AND CALF AT DOUNREAY, CAITHNESS	Pentax 67	165 mm	AP100	F8	1/250	81C
vi	2	SRON NA CREISE, GLENCOE, IN WINTER	Pentax 67	45 mm	AP100	F11	1/60	81A
2	3	LOCH TULLA AND THE BLACKMOUNT	Pentax 67	45 mm	T. Pan	F16	1/15	Orange
4	4	LOCH NA H'ACHLAISE AND RANNOCH MOOR	Wista 5 x 4 in.	90 mm	AP100	F32	1/8	Y/G
6	5	ROCK FORMATIONS, GLEN ETIVE	Linhof 5 x 4 in.	90 mm	FP4	F45	1/4	–
8	6	SRON NA CREISE AND BUCHAILLE ETIVE MOR	Pentax 67	45 mm	AP100	F11	1/30	Orange
10	7	GLENCOE VILLAGE	Pentax 67	45 mm	AP100	F16	1/60	Orange
12	8	CASTLE STALKER, PORTNACROISH	Linhof 5 x 4 in.	90 mm	FP4	F32	1/4	–
14	9	LOCH LINNHE AT AUCHINTORE	Hasselblad	80 mm	Pan F	F16	1/4	–
16	10	BEN NEVIS FROM THE CORPACH BASIN	Pentax 67	45 mm	AP 100	F11	1/60	Orange
18	11	GLENLOCHY DISTILLERY, FORT WILLIAM	Pentax 67	45 mm	AP100	F16	1/4	–
20	12	GLEN NEVIS IN WINTER	Pentax 67	55 mm	AP100	F16	1/4	–
22	13	BEN NEVIS FROM CARN MORE DEARG	Pentax 67	45 mm	AP100	F8	1/125	Orange
24	14	CLEARING LOW PRESSURE, LOCH LOCHY	Wista 5 x 4 in.	90 mm	FP4	F32	1/8	Yellow
26	15	LOCH EILT AND ROIS-BHEINN	Pentax 67	45 mm	AP100	F16	1/15	Y/G
28	16	RIVER AILORT IN WINTER	Pentax 67	55 mm	AP100	F11	1/15	Y/G
30	17	EIGG AND RUM FROM NEAR MALLAIG	Pentax 67	45 mm	AP100	F11	1/125	81A
32	18	MALLAIG AND THE HARBOUR	Pentax 67	165 mm	AP100	F16	1/60	81C
34	19	THE SKYE FERRY LEAVING MALLAIG	Pentax 67	55 mm	AP100	F11	1/60	81A
36	20	CONIFER FOREST IN GLEN GARRY	Pentax 67	300 mm	AP100	F8	1/125	81C
38	21	EILAN DONAN CASTLE, KINTAIL	Pentax 67	165 mm	AP100	F11	1/30	81C
40	22	THE SKYE FERRY AT KYLE OF LOCHALSH	Pentax 67	45 mm	AP100	F11	1/60	81A
42	23	ABANDONED JETTY, LOCH KISHORN	Pentax 67	45 mm	AP100	F11	1/30	Orange
44	24	BEALACH NA BA – THE APPLECROSS PASS	Pentax 67	45 mm	AP100	F11	1/60	81A
46	25	SHIELDAIG, WEST INVERNESS-SHIRE	Pentax 67	165 mm	AP100	F16	1/15	81C
48	26	LOCH MAREE, WESTER ROSS	Pentax 67	45 mm	AP100	F16	1/15	Orange
50	27	FERRY TERMINAL AT ARMADALE, SKYE	Pentax 67	165 mm	AP100	F16	1/60	81C
52	28	SEACLIFFS AT BRAES, SKYE	Hasselblad	50 mm	Pan F	F11	1/30	81A
54	29	THE QUIRANG, STAFFIN, SKYE	Pentax 67	55 mm	AP100	F11	1/30	Orange
56	30	DUIRINISH CHURCHYARD, SKYE	Hasselblad	50 mm	Pan F	F16	1/15	81A
58	31	BLA BHEINN AND CLACH GLAS FROM TORRIN, SKYE	Hasselblad	50 mm	Pan F	F11	1/30	81A
60	32	GARS-BHEINN FROM ELGOL, SKYE	Pentax 67	45 mm	AP100	F16	1/15	Orange
62	33	SGURR NAN GILLEAN, CUILLIN HILLS, SKYE	Nikon F2	24 mm	Pan F	F8	1/60	81A
64	34	LOCH BRITTLE, SKYE	Pentax 67	55 mm	FP4	F11	1/15	–
66	35	THE CUILLIN OF RUM	Linhof 5 x 4 in.	210 mm	FP4	F32	1/4	Orange
68	36	KINLOCH CASTLE, ISLE OF RUM	Linhof 5 x 4 in.	90 mm	FP4	F32	1/2	Y/G
70	37	NORTHERN RAASAY, FROM DUN CAAN	Hasselblad	50 mm	Pan F	F8	1/30	Y/G

PAGE NO.	MAP NO.	TITLE	CAMERA	LENS	FILM	STOP	SPEED	FILTER
72	38	RAASAY HOUSE, CLACHAN BAY	Hasselblad	150 mm	Pan F	F5.6	1/125	–
74	39	THE TORRIDON HILLS FROM LIATHACH	Nikon F2	24 mm	Pan F	F8	1/125	81A
76	40	SHORE STREET, ULLAPOOL, FROM THE PIER	Pentax 67	45 mm	AP100	F11	1/30	Orange
78	41	THE ANCHORAGE, TANERA MORE	Linhof 5 x 4 in.	90 mm	FP4	F22	1/30	
80	42	TANERA MORE AND THE ASSYNT HILLS	Linhof 5 x 4 in.	90 mm	FP4	F32	1/30	Orange
82	43	SUNSET OVER ISLE RISTOL	Linhof 5 x 4 in.	90 mm	FP4	F22	1/60	–
84	44	STAC POLLY, INVERPOLLY NATURE RESERVE	Wista 5 x 4 in.	90 mm	AP100	F32	1/4	Y/G
86	45	CANISP AND SUILVEN	Nikon F2	28 mm	Pan F	F8	1/60	8 1 A
88	46	CHURCH HALL, ELPHIN	Pentax 67	45 mm	AP100	F16	1/15	Red
90	47	THE LEDMORE RIVER NEAR ELPHIN	Pentax 67	45 mm	AP100	F11	1/30	81A
92	48	SHEEP AT LEDMORE JUNCTION	Pentax 67	45 mm	AP100	F11	1/30	81A
94	49	QUINAG, ACROSS LOCH A' CHAIRN BHAIN	Hasselblad	50 mm	Pan F	F16	1/30	–
96	50	LOCH STACK AND THE LAIRG TO LAXFORD ROAD	Linhof 5 x 4 in.	90 mm	FP4	F32	1/4	–
98	51	HEILIM, LOCH ERIBOLL	Pentax 67	90 mm	AP100	F8	1/60	–
100	52	BEACH AT SANGOBEG	Pentax 67	55 mm	AP100	F8	1/60	Orange
102	53	THE FLOW COUNTRY, NEAR KINBRACE	Pentax 67	45 mm	AP100	F16	1/15	81A
104	54	THE RIMSDALE BURN, BADANLOCH	Pentax 67	45 mm	AP100	F11	1/60	–
106	55	THURSO, NEAR COOPER SQUARE	Pentax 67	45 mm	AP100	F11	1/60	81A
108	56	THE HARBOUR, WICK	Pentax 67	45 mm	AP100	F11	1/30	Orange
110	57	THE CAITHNESS COAST AT BERRIEDALE	Linhof 5 x 4 in.	90 mm	FP4	F32	1/4	–
112	58	ROCK SKERRIES NEAR PORTGOWER	Pentax 67	45 mm	AP100	F11	1/125	81A
114	59	ABANDONED BARN, GLEN LOTH	Pentax 67	45 mm	AP100	F11	1/30	Orange
116	60	THE MORAY FIRTH AT LOTH	Pentax 67	45 mm	AP100	F11	1/30	81A
118	61	DUNROBIN CASTLE, GOLSPIE	Pentax 67	55 mm	AP100	F8	1/30	81A
120	62	'PALM BEACH', GOLSPIE, EAST SUTHERLAND	Linhof 5 x 4 in.	90 mm	FP4	F45	1/2	–
122	63	SUNSET OVER LOCH FLEET	Linhof 5 x 4 in.	90 mm	FP4	F32	1/4	–
124	64	THE FREE CHURCH OF SCOTLAND, LAIRG	Pentax 67	45 mm	AP100	F11	1/60	81A
126	65	OIL RIGS IN THE CROMARTY FIRTH	Hasselblad	80 mm	FP4	F5.6	1/250	81A
128	66	URQUHART CASTLE AND LOCH NESS	Pentax 67	45 mm	AP100	F11	1/30	81A
130	67	KESSOCK BRIDGE, INVERNESS	Pentax 67	45 mm	AP100	F11	1/60	81A
132	68	RUTHVEN BARRACKS	Pentax 67	45 mm	AP100	F16	1/15	Y/G
134	69	THE AVIEMORE CENTRE	Pentax 67	45 mm	AP100	F11	1/60	81A
136	70	ROTHIEMURCHUS FOREST NEAR LOCH AN EILAN	Pentax 67	45 mm	AP100	F11	1/15	Y/G
138	71	INSH CHURCH, KINCRAIG	Pentax 67	55 mm	AP100	F16	1/4	Orange
140	72	THE NORTHERN CAIRNGORMS	Nikon F2	28 mm	Pan F	F16	1/15	81A
142	73	BIRCH SAPLINGS, LOCH HOPE	Nikon F2	24 mm	Pan F	F11	1/15	81A